101 WAYS

TO

ENRICH

YOUR

LIFE

*Clear mindsets and simple tools that help you
see everyday experiences in a different way,
and handle them with confidence.*

Robert J. Lemke and Karen K. Diedrich

Living Rich, Inc.
Appleton, Wisconsin

101 WAYS TO ENRICH YOUR LIFE
© COPYRIGHT 1998
by Robert J. Lemke and
Karen K. Diedrich

For information:
Living Rich, Inc.
1724 E. Frances St.
Appleton, WI 54911
www.LivingRich.com

Library of Congress Catalog Card Number: 98-89943

ISBN: 0-9669686-0-3

To our parents:
Jack and Sheila Kuhr,
Norbert and Lora Lemke,
who have enriched our lives
in far more than 101 ways.
Thank you for
believing in us ... always.

Thank You Notes

We are forever grateful to many special people who touch our hearts and influence our thinking. They encourage us to enrich our own lives so that we might help others "live rich" too.

Thank you to our friends, who share our enthusiasm for the Living Rich concepts, and who help us keep moving forward with confidence.

Thank you to the many people we have met in our travels, who put power into these concepts by applying them in everyday life.

Thank you to our families, especially our children, who continue to teach us that loving relationships are our greatest blessing.

Thank you to God, who helps us realize the infinite power of love – the real source of all wealth.

Table of Contents

The Beginning

The young woman was on maternity leave with her infant daughter when she learned that her mother was dying from cancer. The next day, she called her employer to let her bosses know of the situation. That same afternoon, the woman received a call from the company president. He started the conversation by saying simply, "I heard about your mother, and I called because I'm concerned. But I don't know what to say. So how about if you share as much as you're comfortable talking about, and I'll just listen."

The woman began, rather timidly, to share her feelings. She tearfully described what it was like to deal with all of the emotional turmoil and, at the same time, manage the practical aspects of a critical medical situation and a newborn baby. She talked, and she cried. And he listened patiently. She shared her fears and concerns. And he kept listening.

Finally, the president suggested, "You know, I attended a seminar quite recently where I learned: 'The main thing is to keep the main thing the main thing.' If I could offer one bit of help for you, it would be to remember this principle. You have a lot going on right now. Even little things can seem like big things. So it may be helpful to use the 'main thing' expression as a reminder to concentrate on what's really important to you and to avoid worrying too much about everything else."

In the coming months, the woman was able to keep a healthy perspective because she recalled that expression frequently. In fact, she hand-lettered it on a piece of yellow notebook paper, hung it on her refrigerator and read it several times each day.

Cancer tested many things in her life: family relationships, friendships, connections with others in the community, understanding of the medical profession and faith in God. It was a time to question everything, because cancer made it imperative for her to decide what was really important.

Four months later, her mother passed away. And the woman was reminded once again of the power and direction she found in that one, simple "main things" expression.

During the following four years, the woman and the president collected and created many similar expressions. They shared these with family and friends and soon began to train larger groups. They were encouraged when their listeners successfully applied these concepts, and so they wrote a book in order to share their ideas with a wider audience.

You see, the woman and the president are the authors of this book. And the contents are a combination of our shared experiences, favorite expressions and unique perspectives.

In the following chapters, you'll find specific ways of thinking (mindsets) along with simple, practical actions (tools), which can make it easier for you to handle whatever you experience and even to have fun in the process. You'll find ways to manage fear, maintain loving relationships and build your confidence. That's challenging work. And it's a struggle for anyone to implement all of the concepts all of the time. But with each small success you will become more confident and more content. Just keep trying.

And so our fondest wish is that this book presents some memorable and useful principles – and that you find a myriad of ways to truly enrich your life.

MOUNTAINS
AND
MOLEHILLS

Balancing the relative importance of major
things and minor things. Keeping a healthy
perspective. "How you are" with issues,
concerns and priorities.

1.
Align positive beliefs with positive behaviors, and you will be how you really want to be. That's "living rich."

W hat we believe about ourselves directly affects our behaviors. Conversely, how we behave directly affects our beliefs about ourselves. So the objective of "living rich" is to believe good things about ourselves and to choose behaviors which perpetuate those beliefs.

Babies are born into this world with the promise of new life and innocence. We believe in their natural, God-given goodness. They may not be perfect, but they are "perfectly worthy" of being good and becoming even better. Each of us is born with that inherent "goodness." But as we grow, we encounter hurtful situations, disappointments and heartache. It can become difficult to continue to believe that we ARE good and that we can behave well, too. The challenge is to stay focused on our ability to be good and to do good. And when good behaviors support good beliefs about ourselves, then we are living as we are called to live.

The combination of our beliefs and our behaviors is our personal culture. In short, it's "how we are." It's what we show to others, based on what we believe about ourselves. While these beliefs are shaped by many outside influences (parents, teachers, siblings, friends, clergy, etc.), there is also an inner spirit which beckons us to be good and to do good things.

As we mature and become more independent, we have a choice to make. We can continue to let our personal cultures be defined by default. That is, we can allow other people to shape our beliefs about ourselves, thereby also directing our behaviors. Or, we can choose to develop our personal cultures by design. We can consciously choose to believe good things about ourselves, and we can then choose to behave in ways which support those beliefs. Either way, we will get what we expect. But we'll have richer and more fulfilling lives when we take complete responsibility for what we believe and how we behave. When we consciously work to align positive behaviors with positive beliefs, we open ourselves to real joy and real peace. We develop a quiet confidence and a tender courage. We are "rich" when our beliefs and our behaviors are positively aligned.

2.
Stay focused on the mountains,
and you'll keep the molehills
in perspective.

We're often reminded not to make mountains out of molehills. This is generally good advice. However, just as everything should not be mountains, everything should not be molehills either. It is important to have a few mountains in our lives. And mountains deserve far more attention than molehills. Our mountains are our "main things." They're the people and principles about which we feel most strongly. They are critically important to us, in good times and in bad. They keep us pushing forward. They keep us grounded. They're what we stand for and what we believe. They give focus and meaning to our lives.

We have the freedom and the responsibility to consciously choose what will be most important in our lives. When we have determined our mountains, we can make them priorities. When we stay focused on those mountains, we are able to keep the molehills in perspective. But if we see all issues as equally important, then we will give equal attention and energy to them all. And we'll wear ourselves out in the process of tending to them. Is it really right to give equal attention to such unequal issues?

None of us has the time or the energy to treat everything as a mountain. That's why it's so important to keep those molehills small and to make sure they receive appropriately little energy, emotion and concern.

When the molehills tend to escalate, we are challenged to be faithful to our mountains. As we give daily effort and attention to our mountains, we maintain our focus on what we truly value. As long as we are looking toward the mountains, we cannot see the molehills at our feet. When we invest energy into our mountains, the molehills whither away, and we find peace in knowing we have kept perspective.

3.
Visualize your dreams with clarity and detail, and you will be propelled toward making them come true.

If we don't know what we are looking for, how will we know if we find it?

Dreams are mental pictures of how our lives could be. They are the fruits of our imagination. Like pictures on a TV set we see them best when we have tuned them correctly. Adjusting the color and brightness helps us see every detail vividly. Only then can we know what we're really looking at. And only then can we pursue it.

It's exciting to imagine how good life could be ... how good it *will* be. Take some quiet time to think about your heart's desires. Develop the images so you can see them in minute detail and grandiose glory. These thoughts then become the dreams which nourish your soul. They provide the energy that keeps you moving forward. They determine which direction is "forward" for you. They convert your journey from a pleasant wandering to a purposeful mission. They make your life more meaningful and fulfilling.

When we hold dreams that are intense, clear and consistent, we automatically focus in their direction. Our conscious and subconscious thoughts propel our actions toward that destination, and the universe seems to respond by coming to our aid. Dreams really do come true when they are first seen clearly in the mind and then held firmly in the heart.

4.

Listen to your head, trust your instincts and follow your heart.

Our instincts, head and heart are all tools for deciding what is right for us and for helping us become how we really want to be. We need only to use them, and we will find the best answers.

Our heads provide logic – the mechanical and unemotional perspective. Our instincts are the "red flags" or warning signals we sometimes feel in our guts, even when the logic seems sound. Our hearts tell us to be true to our beliefs and to do what we know is right.

Many decisions can be made from a purely logical standpoint. However, when we use logic to talk ourselves into or out of something, it's a clear signal that our instincts, our head and our heart are not in complete agreement. In that case, give the process more time until the right direction becomes evident.

Your head will give you the ability to rationalize just about anything, and your instincts will sometimes present fears. But your heart will always produce the purest response. Your heart will not be misdirected like your ego or your pride. If you find you're using logic to overcome your instincts, or if fear is overcoming your courage, look for the answer in your heart. When in doubt, follow your heart.

5.

Keep a healthy balance between work life and family life, and you'll gain a better perspective on all of life.

How can we keep things in perspective? How can we keep balance in life when we have a demanding job or a challenging personal situation? Look around for role models – other people who have faced similar circumstances and succeeded. What can we learn from someone like Lee Iacocca? He was very successful at Ford and then went on to turn around the entire Chrysler Corporation – and he says he rarely worked on the weekends. Now, if Lee Iacocca could do his job in five days a week, isn't it possible that we could do our jobs and still make time for our family and other interests?

Did you ever see people (usually managers) with "bulging briefcase syndrome?" They put lots of work and reading material into their briefcases, carry it all home, don't touch it that evening, put themselves on a big guilt trip for not doing that work at home, carry it all back to the office the next morning, and then repeat the process that evening. It's better for the psyche if, before leaving the office, you decide what is a reasonable amount of work to do that evening (if any). Then take home only that work and keep your commitment to get that work done. But, while deciding what to take home, remember your other commitments to family, friends, etc. On any given day, you have to decide what is really important, and how you want to spend your time and energy. Your work can be a great source of pleasure and satisfaction. But your work life needn't be your entire life's work.

If you're not sure how much energy to put into something, just ask yourself, "What difference does it really make? How long lasting is the impact of this work? One year from now, when I clean out these files, how important will these issues be then?" It's a question of balance. And in the end, our lives are richer when our passions extend beyond our work.

PERSONAL CULTURE

"How you are." The combination of
your personal beliefs and
behaviors, including your rituals,
ideals and expectations of yourself.

6.

Remember, everything it takes to live rich costs nothing.

L iving rich is aligning positive beliefs with positive behaviors. That process costs nothing. To have positive beliefs about ourselves, and to behave according to those beliefs, is totally independent of our position, possessions, status, or any material things. It simply requires a little time and effort.

Living rich is a balancing act. It is the combination of knowing and accepting ourselves in the present and yet believing that we are still capable of improving. It is the balance between knowing that we are perfectly worthy (even if we're not perfect) and yet wanting to be even better.

When we stay focused on positive beliefs and behaviors, we no longer beat ourselves up for not being "all that we can be" all the time. Additionally, we no longer accept our own inappropriate behavior and use the excuse "that's just how we are." We get off the roller coaster of telling ourselves either that we are really okay, or that we're totally inadequate in some way. Instead, we maintain a constancy of purpose, which allows us to become more peaceful and contented with who we are and how we are.

This is a powerful approach for improving self-esteem, developing strong relationships, becoming more joyful, and accomplishing a personal mission. It helps us find more meaning in life and helps elevate others, too. And, despite all of these positive outcomes, it doesn't cost a penny.

7.
Think about how you want to be and why.

You already have a personal culture. It is the combination of what you believe and how you behave. It's how you are. This culture has been influenced by your own ideas about how you want to be and by the expectations of family, friends, teachers, schoolmates, clergy and others. Therefore, your personal culture has been evolving for a long time. You can decide, however, if it's a culture you want to keep.

Think about how you are and how you want to be. What do you value? What do you believe? Are your behaviors aligned with those beliefs? How do you treat yourself and others? How do you expect to be treated? Are you living according to your own ideals or according to someone else's expectations? Are you comfortable with your choices? When answering these questions, remember that you can accept your culture just as it is, you can modify it, or you can discard it and create a new one. Regardless of the outcome, you will have more confidence in your culture after you have checked it and have consciously decided what is right for you.

By creating a strong personal culture, you ensure that your behaviors embody your beliefs. You become the person you really want to be. You find more strength in your convictions. You feel more centered. And you have the confidence to withstand any pressures to compromise yourself.

8.
Imagine how good it will be to be how you want to be.

O nce you have decided how you want to be, you can create mental images of yourself being that way in all sorts of scenarios. This becomes a "rehearsal" for the actual situations. You know how you will respond because you have already seen it through your mind's eye. You have anticipated the circumstances, practiced responding to them with appropriate feelings and behaviors, and visualized positive outcomes. You have played those scenes over and over in your mind in preparation for actual everyday experiences.

Imagine yourself being peaceful and secure, loving yourself and loving others. Imagine being good to other people and being good to yourself. Imagine having the strength of your convictions and the courage to act on them. Imagine yourself with a real constancy of purpose. Imagine facing even fearful situations with a quiet confidence.

Your mental rehearsal can be preparation for many different experiences in life. In fact, you look forward to them because you're ready. You know how they will look. You know how you will feel. You know how you will be. Your "impromptu" responses have been well rehearsed.

9.

Be how you really want to be; create the life that's right for you.

Focus on being how YOU want to be. Not how your parents think you should be. Or how your boss thinks you should be. Or your children, or your spouse, or your siblings, or your second cousin once removed. Decide what it looks like for you to be a "good person," and then act accordingly.

You can discover what is important to you by examining your passions and your hot buttons – we call them "heart buttons" because they invoke deep feelings and responses. What feels right for you? What are you unwilling to compromise? What is most meaningful to you, even if other important people in your life don't understand or value it? Perhaps you have been taught to "repress" or push down your passions because they were not accepted by other people. You have the opportunity, however, to rediscover and redefine your heart buttons by acknowledging them, studying them and deciding if they are right for you. When you identify your heart buttons and commit yourself to them, it's easy to decide how you should act.

Keep in mind that you can be how you want to be and still show a full range of emotions. For example, you may be quite firm and decisive about your heart buttons. You may be unwilling to compromise on these issues. But, on the other hand, you may be more flexible when it comes to issues that just don't matter so much. So if in the course of a day, you find yourself being calm and gentle and then strong and determined, that's okay. It means that your responses are appropriately situational. The key is to know that, no matter what, you are being true to yourself, and that you're making choices that support your beliefs.

When you really know who you are and you really accept yourself for being how you are, you can be how you want to be. You don't have to give in to outside pressures. You don't have to live your life for anyone else. You can decide how your life is meant to be and create that for yourself.

10.

Work hard to be all that you can be; forgive yourself for what you are not.

It's very noble to strive for perfection and to pursue the quest in that old, familiar commercial from the U.S. Army: "Be all that you can be." On the other hand, we have to be willing to accept that, no matter how hard we try, we will never be perfect in all ways. Everyone has limitations. So, when we don't quite measure up to the standards (our standards or someone else's) the best alternative is to forgive ourselves and move on. The best way to do that is to keep a healthy balance between what we are working on (actions) and how we feel about ourselves as the result of those actions (mindset).

It's typical to think in extremes. On one side is, "I did a good job, so I'm really great," while the other extreme is, "I really goofed up, so I'm no good." There's a huge gap between the two, which can be nearly insurmountable unless we choose, instead, to live peacefully between these extremes.

We are challenged never to accept "that's how I am" as an excuse for giving up too soon or refusing to try to be better. At the same time, we are encouraged to "ease up" on ourselves, to be kinder and gentler with ourselves when our overly critical self-judgments scream silently in our hearts. We need not expect perfection of ourselves, even if that's what we seek. And we can remember that despair is an overreaction to merely being mortal. Be aware of the extremes and walk between them. Keep a high aim tempered by realistic expectations, and you will find peace in that balance.

11.

Generate a healthy balance of passion, productivity and peace; then you will have true power.

Personal power is built on a healthy balance of passion, productivity and peace. These three elements need not be equally proportioned as long as you create the right combination for yourself.

Your "passions" are your heart buttons, your convictions, the people and issues about which you feel strongly. Passions are your burning desires. You are likely to feel strong emotion, enthusiasm and excitement for your passions.

"Productivity" is your work, your output. It requires that you actually DO something. The terms "productivity" or "work" may imply drudgery. But when you feel passionate about something, it's much easier to work hard toward a positive outcome. You're likely to excel in that endeavor. In fact, you may even have fun. Therefore, the combination of passion and productivity is powerful in itself.

"Peace" is rooted in the conscious (and often spiritual) belief that you are "perfectly worthy"– that is, just as worthy as anyone else to feel joy, to succeed, to love and be loved. With that sense of inherent worth comes the belief that your circumstances are okay just as they are or that you are capable of finding a way to make them okay.

This triad of passion, productivity and peace enhances your self-concept and creates an "armor" for you to withstand attacks, setbacks, challenges and hurts. This personal power keeps you focused on doing the right thing, even when that is difficult. It helps you love and accept yourself, regardless of a bad day at the office or a fight with your teenager. It keeps you "centered" and grounded in your beliefs, even when others pass judgment or try to convince you that you should change. Personal power adds meaning to your passions, momentum to your work and depth to your peace.

12.
Don't let fear keep you from daring to live the life you dream.

I magine that you already have decided what kind of life you desire. You have thought about how you want to be, what you hope to do and what "creature comforts" you might like. You have created a picture of how your life could be, and you clearly see all the rewards that life would provide. Sounds great in theory, but you still face a major obstacle – fear. When you are intimidated by your fears, you surrender the power of your dreams. When you acknowledge your fears and forge ahead anyway, you greatly increase the potential to live a richer life.

Picture yourself walking barefoot through the grass. Then, without warning, you step on a sharp pebble. It hurts. And it's appropriate for you to acknowledge that hurt. Immediately, your instincts tell you to protect yourself from feeling that kind of pain again. But don't put your shoes back on. Instead, keep walking barefoot. You may risk some minor pain, but in the meantime, you are promised the pleasure of feeling the soft grass under your feet. The moral of the story: It's better to risk stepping on a pebble occasionally than to wrap your shoes so tightly around your feet that you never experience the sensual, barefoot walk which you originally desired. So it is with dreams. When you seek positive outcomes you must also accept the risks and fears which accompany those rewards.

Remember that everyone has fears. Even the people who appear to be most successful and admired have had to overcome some fears. So assume the mindset that you can overcome your fears too. When you focus on the life you want, you will tighten the grip on your dreams and loosen the stranglehold of your fears.

13.

Make sure that what you say to yourself is as charitable as what you say to others.

There's a very powerful tool in sometimes thinking of yourself as a third person. It allows you to treat your "self" with the same courtesy and respect that you extend to others.

Imagine that a close friend just made a mistake and is now confiding in you. You listen to the pain and the remorse as your friend laments the situation. What would you tell that friend? Wouldn't you extend empathy and understanding? Wouldn't you gently and kindly encourage your friend to accept minor imperfections and try forgiveness instead of self-punishment? Wouldn't you feel that your friend is being far more critical than anyone else would be?

The next time you are not perfect and you're tempted to call your "self" names or put your "self" down, please tell your "self" that you are perfectly worthy just the way you are. You're okay even if you aren't "all that you can be" every minute of every day. It's more important to work on the upward spiral of "being how you want to be" and forgiving yourself when you make a mistake along the way.

Be as good to yourself as you would be to your best friend. And remember that the words you say to yourself can be the most helpful or the most harmful – even if you're the only one who hears them.

14.
Keep your self-worth separate from your net worth.

O ur self-worth and our net worth are totally independent of each other. But in this very materialistic society, it can become easy to confuse the two. We are sometimes tempted to measure ourselves in terms of lifestyles, possessions or dollars. And, while those things are understandably valued, it's important also to weigh our worth in terms of character. After all, would you prefer that people talk about what possessions you have or what kind of person you are?

Net worth is easy to identify and calculate. An accountant can quickly determine someone's net worth and help plan ways to use existing assets to make even more money. But money is very fickle. People gain and lose fortunes every day. If we tie our self-worth to our net worth and we lose our net worth, what do we have left? Regardless of whether our net worth goes up or down, we're better off to measure our self-worth on it's own curve.

Self-worth can be a little more difficult to define and develop than net worth. However, we can practice positive beliefs and behaviors to generate and enhance our self-esteem, regardless of what a bank statement says. For example, we can take pride in being how we want to be and in doing the right thing. We can enjoy the pursuit of our passions and the strength of our convictions. We can be comfortable with ourselves and be good to ourselves (and to others). These sources of self-worth are enduring. And in the end, they can influence our health, peace of mind and quality of life far more than money ever could.

It's possible to have megabucks and feel tormented. It's possible to have very little money and still "live rich." (Or it might be really nice to have a wonderful life AND lots of money.) But net worth and a bank account have nothing to do with how much we "count" in this world. The real worth of a person and how that person impacts others cannot be measured in dollars.

15.

Take complete responsibility
for your own happiness.
(This means you "own" your
unhappiness, too.)

O ne of the best ways to drive home this message is through a simple conversation. Try this some time: When someone is complaining to you about something, say, "You really seem unhappy about that." And the other person is likely to say, "Oh yes, I am." Then you can respond, "Well, who do you think is responsible for your happiness?" Typically the other person will quickly come to the inescapable conclusion and state, "I guess I am."

We each have the right to pursue happiness. We also have a responsibility for that happiness. So if we don't get what we want, it's not necessarily someone else's fault. Many of us are tempted to think that "bad things" always happen to us. It's as though a black cloud follows us everywhere and rains on us continually. Sometimes it feels like we are the only people in the world who get flat tires, who have stressful family relations, or who miss the last train to Clarksville.

Truth is, other people and unrelated circumstances don't have to affect our happiness. In fact, no one else can make us happy or unhappy. We each have the ability, and the responsibility, to take charge of our happiness. We can choose to fuss about a situation, or we can make the most of it. We can choose to say it was "a bad day," or we can say that "some yucky stuff happened inside a good day."

How many days of your life are you willing to write off as bad days? How much of your potential happiness are you willing to delegate to someone else? When we take responsibility for our current and continued happiness, we become less bitter and demanding. We move from hand-wringing to action, which helps us become more content with our current situation. And as a result, other people become more content with us.

16.
View happiness as a continuum rather than a toggle switch.

Instead of questioning whether or not you are happy, try asking how happy you are. This shifts your perception of happiness. Instead of viewing it as a switch that is either on or off, you can see it as a knob that has a wide range of adjustment.

To ask, "How happy am I?" is to assume that you are at least partially happy. This allows for even greater happiness since it's much easier to build on "some" happiness than to create "some" from "none," or to eliminate unhappiness.

Even in times of sorrow, it is possible to find moments of happiness. In fact, it's spiritually nourishing to find bits of humor or to create small celebrations during difficult times or grief. To acknowledge any happiness when you would otherwise feel despair is to see that the proverbial cup is at least partially full. (And even to recognize that there IS a cup.) This belief breeds hope.

Mentally place yourself on the continuum to reinforce that your happiness does not turn "off" and "on" from moment to moment or day to day. You will better appreciate whatever happiness you already enjoy, develop confidence that the next negative thing won't switch you over to "unhappy," and recognize the potential to become even happier.

17.
Look for joy when sharing chores as much as when sharing leisure.

We tend to think of chores as "no fun" and leisure as "all fun." Leisure, then, becomes an infrequent reward for all of our hard work. When we consider how much time we spend at work and doing chores, compared with how little time is left for leisure, wouldn't it be a shame to spend so much of our lives in the absence of joy?

Joy tends to be elusive because of the way we think about it. We expect that joy will suddenly appear or that we will stumble upon it, and then we'll be pleased with its unanticipated presence. We hope that we will simply "feel it" someday (usually far off in the future) after the mortgage is paid, the kids are grown, the house is furnished, the cars are fixed and our lives are "in order."

Don't wait for joy to come knocking. You can seek out joy at any time under any circumstances. You can find joy the same way you would find anything else – just look for it! When you look for joy, you will find it, even in the midst of work.

18.
Address your "inside" needs on the inside.

Nothing from the outside can make you feel emotionally or spiritually full on the inside. When your heart is empty, when you feel emotionally empty, remember that you can't fill up your heart with food, alcohol, shopping, work, fancy cars, big houses, etc. Address your real needs. Look inside yourself and try to figure out what is really missing. Are you feeling unfulfilled, unimportant, unworthy, un-something?

When we're hungry, we eat. We try to fill up. If we still don't feel full, we eat more. Unfortunately, we tend to address matters of the heart in the same way. We try to develop some external fix, and when it doesn't work well enough to resolve the issue, we go for more of that fix or a bigger variety of fixes.

It's a rude awakening when you find yourself in a poorer position from trying to get yourself into a better position, but by using the wrong means. Save yourself the heartache of looking in all the wrong places. Start looking on the inside. What would make you feel better about yourself? Many people improve their self-image by changing only two or three small things, like doing some volunteer work, losing some weight, getting more organized, pursuing more education, or reconnecting with family and friends. No amount of money, no fashionable shoes, no shiny trophy can make you feel good about yourself for very long. Emotional and spiritual fulfillment has to come from within.

19.
Value contrasts,
especially in yourself.

C ontrasts within a person are a sign of strength. It can be desirable to be strong yet gentle, outgoing yet introspective, logical yet intuitive. In fact, such diversity helps us keep a reasonable balance in our outlook and act appropriately as different situations require. It's possible to be a good talker AND a good listener, for example.

We limit ourselves when we label ourselves with expressions like, "I'm not very good at _____." Saying (and believing) those kinds of things makes it sound like we've given up – we've resolved ourselves to not being very good in certain areas. We can choose, instead, to view those areas as simply "underdeveloped." This will change our mindset from "surrender" to "taking charge."

We all have a few characteristics which are unchangeable (like eye color, height and shoe size). Numerous other qualities and behaviors are learned, which means they can be changed. Are there things you would like to change from underdeveloped to at least satisfactory? If so, start telling yourself, "I'm pretty good at _____," and start practicing. You will find you can make substantial improvement in a short time. We don't need to accept that we're not good enough at something and then resign ourselves to that condition. As human beings, we have a multitude of feelings, personality traits and character elements. And we're capable of becoming far more diverse than we realize.

20.
Good people attract good people. So be good people.

If you want the people around you to be good people, then you have to be a good person first. You set the standard. Then lead by example. And others will follow.

You don't have to be perfect. You will meet or exceed most standards if you are consistently reliable, responsible, respectful and trustworthy – RRRT. (See Number 67.) This applies at home, at work and everywhere else. You can't fix the whole world, but you're surrounded by people you can influence. Start with yourself. Focus on the RRRT guideposts and you'll be amazed how good people are drawn to you, as you are to them.

21.
Open yourself up
to opportunity.
It's all around you.

This is a mindset of optimism. It is the belief that opportunity is everywhere. When we adopt this belief, we become more aware of what is occurring all around us, even if none of it seems especially relevant at the moment. Then, regardless of how focused we already are on specific goals and activities, we are also mindful that other options exist and could be even better.

Try to stay keenly aware of what is happening all around you. Keep an open mind, so you can be receptive to new information. And be ready to alter your course when the inputs are telling you that a different direction offers greater opportunity.

22.

Believe in yourself; invest in yourself; gamble on yourself.

While statements like this are frequently intended for entrepreneurs, this concept is meaningful for everyone. You can go to a casino and gamble that you will make big money. Or you can invest only in someone else's ideas or business. But why not spend some money on your own self-development and invest in your own future?

Perhaps you would like to further your education, pursue an avocation more seriously or test a new business theory. If you have a dream you are longing to pursue, start by believing in yourself and your ability to determine what's right for you. If you first believe in yourself, you will be more willing to invest in yourself and even to take a gamble on yourself.

23.
Embrace change as you did when you were a child.

L ittle children are really good examples for us to follow. Their whole world changes whenever they learn a new skill – like walking, talking or feeding themselves. Children typically can't wait until they're "big enough" or "old enough" to learn something new and become more independent. Clearly, each change inspires growth – mentally, physically, emotionally and spiritually.

Change also inspires fear, especially as we age. Think back to all the changes you've encountered as you've matured and how scary they seemed at the time. In retrospect, you may see that "everything worked out in the end," but it is difficult to have that attitude when you don't know what "the end" will look like.

The best approach for dealing with change as an adult is to get information and then take action. (After all, the only difference between a hard question and an easy one is whether or not you know the answer.) So learn as much as you can about what is changing, why the change is needed and how the new course of action could improve the situation. Of all the questions, the most important is WHY. You can't support a change if you don't understand why it's happening. If no one will give you this information, try to find your own answers before taking action.

After you have gathered the information, and assuming you can support the benefits of the change, then you are prepared to embrace that change and grow with it. Together, information and action will help to dissipate the fears you might have had, and you might even find yourself being enthusiastic about the entire new endeavor. Change inspires growth.

24.

Don't let anyone burst your bubble or steal your dreams.

You have an extraordinary ability to choose what is right for you. Don't be intimidated out of pursuing positive dreams. There are many naysayers in this world who seem eager to point out all the possible problems you could have with any chosen path. But if you've gathered enough relevant information, if you're following your heart, and if you believe that this is truly the right thing for you at this time, then go for it. Give yourself a chance to succeed and to live the life you dream. Don't let other people's fears, or even good intentions, prevent you from making your own choices. It's a very hollow existence if you sacrifice your own aspirations in order to meet everyone else's expectations.

Be cautioned that family and friends may have advice worth heeding. It's always worthwhile to listen carefully (at least initially) to what others tell you. But if it becomes clear that the intent is not to help you, but to hold you back, then it's time to move on. Smile pleasantly, thank them for their input, but don't let it affect your decision.

25.
Decide for yourself
what you believe.

Have you ever felt an internal conflict because you were doing something that you thought other people wanted, but it wasn't what you really wanted? Have you ever said "yes" to a request when you wished you had found the courage to say "no" gracefully? Have you perpetuated family traditions out of habit, or fear, even if they no longer seemed appropriate for you?

We tend to follow these same old behaviors (even when we don't like them) unless we have given serious thought to our belief systems and consciously chosen the right values for ourselves. Therefore, the first challenge is to decide what we really believe and focus on developing positive beliefs. Then we can begin to behave in ways which support those beliefs. We can make the best choices for ourselves, regardless of what anyone else might think, say or do. When our behaviors are aligned with our beliefs, internal conflict is reduced.

In the end, it doesn't make a lot of difference if you're in total agreement with everyone else around you. What matters most is that you know your own mind and follow your own heart. Then you will become less threatened by opposing beliefs. You will become less judgmental of different behaviors. You will become more tolerant of others and more accepting of yourself.

26.
Stand on a soapbox and tell others what you believe.

When you figuratively "step up onto a soapbox" in front of family, friends, co-workers, etc., you take the opportunity to share your feelings and beliefs. If you have determined what you believe, then go ahead and share your philosophies with others. Initially you will feel more strength in your convictions simply because you are stating them aloud. Other people may not agree with you, but at least they will know where you stand. Additionally, your words become a window to your character. When you explain who you are and how you are, you build opportunities for meaningful relationships with other people. When strong personal cultures are expressed and shared, they become the foundation for strong interpersonal cultures.

27.

Find the right guiding principles to live by, and the individual decisions will be easy.

When even a small decision feels like a big dilemma, ask yourself, "What is the guiding principle for this decision?" If you know your own philosophies and principles, it's easy to do a quick check of specific actions to see if they are within your general standards of behavior.

For example, some people abide by the principle that they will not make a major purchase without considering it carefully for at least 24 hours. Then, when they experience high-pressure sales tactics ("Would you take it today if I could get my boss to reduce the price by $100?") the answer is easy. They simply respond, "No, I always sleep on these decisions before I commit to a purchase of this magnitude." The sales people relent because they know the buyer won't budge. The process works!

Whenever you base your lower-level decisions on your higher-level principles, you will find it amazingly easy to stay within your own "hallways of behavior," no matter what the topic. If you value relationships, then you might follow the rule that you will always treat people with respect and dignity. You know immediately which behaviors are acceptable and which behaviors you will not even consider. No fretting, no agonizing, no deliberation required.

It's worth the time and effort invested "up front" to become clear and firm about your guiding principles because then the detailed decisions will become almost automatic. As a result, you'll be consistently true to your own standards. And, you'll be much less tempted to compromise yourself or to "sell your soul"– not even to rent it out!

28.

Do what you know is right, even if there are fools in your world who try to convince you otherwise.

By simple definition, fools* in your world act unwisely or imprudently, as evaluated against your standards. Therefore, they don't have much credibility with you. Yet they are likely to be rather vocal about your decisions and actions.

Perhaps you have tried to live according to high values, only to have fools point out what you "should have" done. Perhaps fools have passed judgment on you or your decisions, when they didn't even know you or have any of the information you had. These people can push you to the point of wanting to stop doing the right and principled things because they make the process so painful for you.

Think of the fools in your world. Try to list them by name. Then do some quick soul-searching. If you already consider their behavior to be foolish, then why would you allow them to intimidate you? If they have low credibility, then why would you be concerned with what they might say? If they share similar traits like pessimism, sarcasm or cynicism, then why would you expect them to support your decisions? In this context, the direction becomes quite clear: Don't try to be perfect to please the fools in your world, and don't try to debate them. You can instead, simply choose to remind yourself that you don't value their opinions on other topics, so their opinions about you and your decisions aren't relevant for you, either.

If at all possible, find a way to value the positive things these people do contribute, and try to ignore the rest of their behaviors. When you develop this mindset, you regain the resolve to do what you know is right.

*PLEASE NOTE: The term "fool" is used only to describe people who portray foolish behavior, based on your standards. It is not intended to describe a whole person or group of people. In this context, there are no value judgments placed on anyone.

29.
Do the right thing, even when you're afraid.

When someone appears to be very courageous, we tend to think they must be fearless. Conversely, we may think that if we feel fear within ourselves we must be cowardly.

In reality, we all have fears. AND we all have courage. It's not an either/or situation. But the differentiating factor is that courageous people forge ahead and do the right thing, even when they're afraid.

Mark Twain said that courage is not the absence of fear. How encouraging! We don't have to conquer all fear in order to summon the courage already rooted in our passions and convictions. When we focus on courage, we become more courageous. We can identify and acknowledge fears, but act in spite of them.

30.
Take a stand, even if you stand alone.

It's easy to do the right thing when we're surrounded by others who support us and stand with us. It's much more challenging, however, to do the right thing and to publicly take a stand when we know we may stand alone. These are our moments of truth. These are the times when we weigh the depth of our passions against the pressure of our peers.

You must decide what is best for you. You can follow the leader or follow your heart. But keep in mind that you will always find the courage to stand alone if your actions are based on your principles and convictions. And when you take a stand, you strengthen your personal culture – no matter how popular or unpopular your position.

31.
Try to learn something from everyone you meet.

Regardless of your background, intelligence, education and experience, you can learn something from everyone you meet. Only two things are required: First, you need to focus more on listening than on talking. And second, you need to have a desire to learn rather than a desire to impress.

Even when you don't "click" with someone right away, it's possible to stay engaged in the conversation, to ask questions and to listen long enough to learn something. And if you're focused on learning, you will automatically become less focused on impressing. It's so much more interesting and fulfilling to go through life trying to learn from others, rather than trying to show others what you know.

Just listen, really listen, and you will learn something from everyone.

32.

Make a habit of teaching the things you most want to learn.

How do you teach something if you haven't learned it? It's in the process of preparing to teach that you really learn the material. Preparation requires that you study the topic, organize your thoughts and learn the details so well that you can present them to others.

The best teachers, coaches and mentors are excited about their roles because they are focusing on the topics they want to learn about, think about and talk about with others. They are teaching what they like best. They have discovered the knowledge or skills that work for them, and now they're sharing that information with the hope that it will help someone else.

Nearly every day you'll find "teachable moments" with children, siblings, co-workers or friends. And each time you share your learnings, ideas and principles, you reinforce them for yourself. When teaching, you make a meaningful contribution by helping others. You feel good about yourself. And you discover how much you have yet to learn.

33.
Think of everything, especially the difficult times, as preparation for the future.

It's easy to get caught in a downward spiral if you focus too much on the challenges and stresses in your life. It's tempting to become a martyr, to think that everyone else has it so much better. And it can be difficult to climb back out of that emotional vortex.

When you focus on how a difficulty is preparing you for something in the future, you gain a more positive perspective. You begin to see the value of it, even if you don't appreciate it. You start to think about what you're learning from this experience. And you move from hand wringing to action planning. When you move from the state of not knowing what to do, to the state of planning a specific, positive action, then you regain momentum and are able to move forward again.

If you look back over your personal history, you'll probably find that after each deeply challenging situation, you experienced some sort of "quantum leap" that changed your perspective or actions and propelled you forward. These are usually the moments of profound change in one's thought patterns, emotional responses and spirituality.

Once you recognize the pattern of trials-leading-to-growth, it's easier to accept whatever your current situation is, because you know that something good can and will result.

34.
Do things which will earn you respect (for your character) instead of doing things which will get you liked (for your personality).

If the motive behind your actions is to gain popularity, you will undoubtedly compromise your values somewhere along the line. When you tell people what you think they want to hear, you lose track of the truth. When you succumb to peer pressure, you lose the ability to stand on principle even if you stand alone. (See Number 30.) Popularity is about personality. It pays no regard to the real substance of a person.

Character, on the other hand, is your personal bedrock. It requires that you take the high road, tell the truth and do the right thing, even though people may not always like you for it. With a strong character, you can earn respect even in the absence of popularity.

It's very possible for people to respect you without liking you. But they can never really like you without respecting you first. So work from your character. Focus on gaining respect by doing what you think is right. Don't worry too much about how well people like you. If you earn respect first, popularity will follow in due season.

35.
Behave as though your parents and your children are watching.

A ssuming your parents and children (if you have children) are important to you, they're very likely to see "the real you." They know how you are regardless of your job title, income, net worth, possessions or other "trappings." There's no need to impress them, yet people generally do want to put their best foot forward for family.

Family members typically want you to be the best person you can be. They're on your side, but they will also hold you to your own high standards of behavior. If you behave as though they're watching, then you're likely to behave with high character, even when they're not around.

INTERPERSONAL CULTURE

Relationships built upon shared beliefs and behaviors. The customs, traditions and practices you share with family, friends, co-workers, acquaintances, etc.
"How you are" with other people.

36.
Encourage others to be how they want to be.

When individuals with strong personal cultures join together, they have the foundation to build a powerful interpersonal culture. Once established, an interpersonal culture is best nurtured when both parties continue to be how they want to be while also encouraging each other to do the same.

To encourage is to inspire or impart courage – to help others discover that they do, in fact, have courage. It does not mean that you merely share a positive mental attitude, or that you become a cheerleader. It requires, instead, that you take a more subtle approach. To encourage is to gently nudge, mildly suggest, continually plant the seeds that inspire new thoughts and perspectives. It's mentoring without lecturing, questioning without intimidating, developing without demanding.

Those who encourage become advocates and safety nets for others. They supply the logic or the emotion that you may be needing at the moment. For example, they may politely suggest that you're trying to make a decision without enough information. Or they may help you develop deep feelings and passionate pursuits. They challenge you to consider the future effects of your behavior when you are considering inappropriate actions. They become a "safe place" for you to vent your frustrations and to be less than perfect, while reminding you that you are still perfectly worthy.

When you share encouragement with others, you also share in their success. You expand your focus to include a broader audience. You become less concerned with your own trials and tribulations. You build deep, long-lasting relationships based on mutual support and acceptance. You build your own personal culture because you become more of how you want to be.

37.
Look for the good in people.

It's easy to see what you don't like, what irritates you, what threatens you. It's habit forming to complain and criticize others in order to "build up" yourself. If you go through life thinking that nearly everyone is a jerk, you're going to meet quite a few jerks. When you start looking for the good in people, you're going to find an abundance of wonderful people. When you change your perception, you change your reality. That's why you're likely to find whatever it is you seek.

What do you look for when you receive a performance review or some other type of feedback such as "helpful" advice from someone who is "only telling you this because they're your friend"? Do you tend to focus on the positive comments, or do you zoom in on a few less-than-perfect scores and give them far more attention than they deserve? So it is with relationships. Do you focus on people's positive qualities or do you magnify small peculiarities and imperfections? Do you make it a habit to attack or do you make it a habit to appreciate?

We all get back whatever we give. When we give kindness, we find it. When we give love, we receive it. When we look for the good in other people, we become better ourselves.

38.
Always try to protect the dignity of others.

To protect others' dignity is to acknowledge their inherent worth, and to avoid games of one-upmanship. Do not trod on others or "rub their noses" in anything – even if you don't agree with them, even if they've hurt you, even if they have been disrespectful to you. Protect their dignity because it's the right thing to do.

Questions of dignity arise not only with "big incidents" (like employment terminations), but also with "daily details" (like when someone spills something on you or calls you by the wrong name). You can choose to embarrass other people and belittle them, or you can protect their dignity by discretely helping them to adjust, changing the subject, or simply ignoring the issue and refraining from comment.

Be careful, however, not to sacrifice your own dignity in order to protect another's. There's no such thing as a dignified doormat. Try to practice respect for yourself and for others. Treat people like the good people they are – even if they are experiencing a bit of misfortune.

39.
Don't reject people totally, just because you can't condone some of their behaviors.

Sometimes people behave in ways we simply cannot condone. Just because we find the behavior unacceptable, however, does not mean that we have to find the person unacceptable. Don't confuse the person with the behavior. And don't condemn a person because of random acts of behavior.

All of us behave inappropriately at times. That doesn't mean we are "bad" people. It just means that we make mistakes. However, we frequently view someone else's mistakes in an exaggerated way and begin to identify – and even label – those people according to their behaviors. For example, have you ever heard someone called a "naughty boy" because he spilled milk, broke a toy or threw a tantrum? His behaviors may seem naughty, but he is not naughty. Similarly, you may have heard someone called a "dummy" because he didn't have the information to answer a specific question. It's a blow to people's self-esteem when we label them in these ways. And that punishment is far too severe for the "crime."

If someone is misbehaving, you can accept it, you can ignore it or you can try to change it. No matter which approach you choose, try to keep the mindset that you can dislike the behavior and still accept and value the person.

40.
Be aware of the power of your words. Say things that feather people's wings, not heavy their hearts.

It is said that actions speak louder than words. But words do have the power to build people up or to tear them down – sometimes irrevocably.

Other people may remember what we say long after we've forgotten the entire conversation. Why? Because our words influence their thoughts. And when our words influence their thoughts about themselves (their self-image), we either feather their wings with encouragement or we heavy their hearts with doubt. There is no possible gain in heavying a heart through our sarcasm, criticism, cynicism or other verbal abuse. It's hurtful to others and to ourselves.

Choose your words carefully. Speak kindly *to* others and *to* yourself. Speak kindly *about* others and *about* yourself. Wield the power of your words with discretion.

41.

It's better to compliment someone's character than to compliment things like appearance, achievement or ability.

C haracter issues are more relevant in the long term than are things like appearance, achievement and ability. People can influence their characters far more than their inherited abilities or physical traits. The most meaningful compliments focus on character.

Say, for example, a child studies very hard for an exam and gets an "A" on it. We typically would comment on the child's intelligence or the grade. ("Oh Suzy, you're so smart," or "Wow, you got the best grade in the class.") The character issues, however, are that Suzy developed a good work ethic and took the responsibility to work up to her potential. When we compliment Suzy for these behaviors, we reinforce their long-term value, as opposed to Suzy's inherited intelligence or grade on one small test.

Similarly, it's better to compliment Suzy's ability to take a stand, than to compliment the fact that she is tall when she stands. Her height is inherited. She has no control over it. If we tell her how pleased we are that she is the tallest in her class, our comments will ring hollow if later she is passed up by her classmates.

Compliments guide behaviors. Compliments are positive feedback that promote more of a desirable behavior. When we compliment character, we encourage others to be of high character. While compliments on achievements or ability are sure to be appreciated, they are weaker compliments because they focus on what people do and how people look, rather than how people are.

42.

Remember that negative comments about other people are like grass seeds scattered in the wind. They can never be recovered, yet they quickly take root in the hearts and minds of others.

G rass seeds are very fine and lightweight. They scatter easily. And once scattered in the wind, they are virtually impossible to recover or collect. When they fall to the ground they root and begin to grow quickly, even in unfavorable conditions.

So it is with our words – especially our negative words. They fly from our tongues with little effort. They are spread easily among other people. And they influence the mind and heart of each person who hears them. Nasty comments, hurtful judgments, rumors and innuendo can never be fully retrieved.

Be mindful of what you say. Be careful that you plant only the seeds from which you would truly like to harvest.

43.
Don't miss an opportunity to say something nice.

How many complimentary things do we think, but not say? Do we fear rejection if we say something nice? Do we think it's not important to make the effort? Regardless of your personal reasons, you can easily share more compliments by adopting the simple mindset: Tell people what you like about them. When you think nice things about others, ask yourself, "Have I told them that?" When someone tells you how much they appreciate something that a third person did, simply ask, "Have you told them that?"

While it may be fairly easy to compliment someone's shoes or haircut, we are generally not in the habit of commenting directly to people about their beliefs and behaviors – the more meaningful issues. It may take some effort to tell someone, "I was really impressed with the way you stuck up for that little boy who was being bullied on the school bus today." If you find the courage to say it, you'll be encouraged and so will the receiver! It's a little way to make a big difference.

With each compliment you show appreciation, shine a little light and build better relationships. Tell people what you like about them. Call them on the phone, write a short note, send an e-mail or tell them in person. It's not important which medium you use. Just tell them.

44.
Vow to never consciously hurt another human being and TELL people that.

When you make a commitment like this, you clearly define how you want to behave. You strengthen your personal culture. When you tell others that you have made this promise to yourself, you make it clear how you want to behave toward them. You strengthen your interpersonal culture with them.

Once you explain that you would never intentionally hurt other people, they begin to trust that any hurt you may subsequently cause them must be inadvertent. They will give you the benefit of the doubt because they know that you are well intentioned even if you make a mistake. With that understanding, it becomes safe for them to talk with you about hurt feelings. Together you can discuss your behavior, deal with the misunderstandings and move on. When people know how you're trying to be, they'll work harder to understand your behavior and to protect the relationship.

45.
Treat other people's possessions with as much respect as they do.

Relationships are easily damaged if we don't treat other people's possessions with at least the same respect as they do. When we're disrespectful of someone's possessions, we send the unspoken message that we don't respect the owner either. The relationship is immediately threatened. Therefore, the respect with which we treat a person's possessions is a clear reflection of the respect we feel for the person. It's not about things. It's about relationships.

Perhaps you have neighbors or siblings who are quite particular about their possessions. If you use or borrow something of theirs, or even ride in their vehicles, you are obliged to treat their possessions as they would. Even if your standards are more relaxed, it's best to meet their standards when using their things. If "good enough" for you is not "good enough" for them, take extra caution to abide by their standards. Remember that the way you treat other people's possessions will either protect or damage your relationships.

46.
Look for opportunities to do favors for others.

You generate deeper connections with other people when you invest a bit of your time, talent or energy by doing small favors for them. And you benefit in three ways: Other people feel good about you; you feel good about yourself; and, surprisingly, you feel better about the other people! Look for opportunities to help other people, even those you're not especially fond of. You'll like them (and yourself) better.

47.

When someone does you a favor, accept it graciously and pass it on.

It can feel awkward to accept favors from others, especially if we feel unworthy of the kindness. It's important to remember, however, that in our hesitancy we may deprive people of doing good things for us. It's beneficial for both parties when we can graciously accept favors.

We may offer to pay for the favor or to repay the favor. Under many circumstances, however, the giver might be insulted by such suggestions. In any case, keep in mind that there will always be an opportunity, somewhere along the line, to pass the favor on.

There's tremendous power in passing it on. We are reminded of the initial favor. We have the pleasure of perpetuating the process by teaching others to be open to kindness and eager to share it. We build interpersonal cultures of generosity.

48.
Ask for help when you need it, and accept it when people offer it to you.

E verybody needs a little help now and then. It can be scary to realize that we're mere mortals who don't "know it all" and can't "do it all." It's a humbling experience to discover that we can't be all things to all people, despite the pride which frequently tries to convince us otherwise. It's very liberating to stop struggling alone and let someone else share a burden. And, it can be a big relief just to get past the fear of asking for help.

It may feel like we're prevailing upon others when asking for their help. However, most people need to be needed, at least occasionally, and they are typically willing to help. In fact, good friends want to help because it strengthens the relationship. They have a stake in our happiness, as we do in theirs.

No matter how willing they are, other people can only give us as much help as we're willing to accept. If we believe that we don't deserve it, then we won't take it even though others offer it. When we realize that we're worthy of help, and others want to help, then we can accept it graciously. We become thankful that we asked and that our friends delivered. No one has to struggle alone. Let people help, and be willing to return the favor.

49.
Don't lose too much sleep over what someone else has said.

How much time do you spend worrying about what someone else has said to you? Does the idea of constructive criticism send your mind reeling? Are performance evaluations your idea of slow and painful torture? Have you spent days feeling hurt or angry because of a minor disagreement or misunderstanding? Have you lost a night's sleep because someone made a hurtful comment? In retrospect, how much of your time have you spent in agony? And how much of your agony has been for naught?

More than anything, this concept is intended to help you keep a healthy and positive perspective. Next time you're staring at the ceiling in the middle of the night because someone's words have heavied your heart, take a minute to imagine the "perpetrator" sleeping blissfully. It's likely, after all, that while you're lying there fretfully, they're dreaming peacefully. Ask yourself, "Do I really want to spend my time and energy like this?" If you decide "no," then you're ready to move to positive action.

In virtually every case, you have three choices: Accept it, change it or reject it. Try to recall exactly what was said to you and then decide if it has merit. If so, decide how you will use the comments to modify your beliefs or behaviors. If there's no merit in the comments, reject them completely. Then focus on the personal and interpersonal cultures you value, and get a good night's sleep.

50.
Physically remove yourself from the few people who don't want you to be the best you can be.

A mong the people you know and love, there may be a minimal portion (say 5%) who don't seem to have your best interest at heart. These may be the people who consistently nibble at your self-image by criticizing you, refusing to share your joys and discouraging you from following your dreams. They invoke fear rather than inspire courage. They may say they care about you when actually they are threatened by you or competing with you. Regardless of their motives, you know the outcomes. Your relationships with these people are not healthy. They can have a devastating effect on your self-image unless you have a personal culture strong enough to withstand their insidious harm.

Your best response is to protect yourself and distance yourself. This requires that you be assertive in your discussions and interactions, even to the point of physically removing yourself. It takes courage to change or end relationships. Although you may initially grieve the loss, you free yourself to invest emotion and energy into other relationships that are more nurturing and fulfilling.

LOVING
RELATIONSHIPS

51.
Build and keep relationships that are:

Calm

Loving

Open

Safe

Empathic

The elements of CLOSE are the foundation for loving relationships, the strongest and most positive interpersonal cultures. You can use CLOSE as a figurative checklist to determine if your relationships are on the right track:

C alm — peaceful and relaxed; free of tension.

L oving — affectionate, caring and nurturing.

O pen — receptive and respectful; showing emotion.

S afe — free of fear and danger; secure and forgiving.

E mpathic — a state of understanding; feeling what your partner feels without passing judgment or giving advice.

Take responsibility for creating and maintaining an environment that is calm, loving, open, safe and empathic. Build loving relationships with people who share your desire to make CLOSE a priority.

52.
Accept yourself
unconditionally.

Book store shelves are full of self-help manuals dedicated entirely to this subject. Some people delve into this material with keen interest, while others find it downright frightening. If you want to enrich your life by practicing unconditional acceptance of yourself and others, it's easy to get started with the simple mindset: "I'm okay."

Maybe you can't figure out why the car is making that funny clunking sound, or maybe your creative abilities with arts and crafts aren't comparable to Martha Stewart's. But you're okay. Maybe you're not in the ideal job or the ideal marriage. But you're okay. Maybe you're not perfect. But you're okay.

Once you have this mindset of self-acceptance, you can improve your ability to love unconditionally by using the tools of a strong personal culture: Align positive behaviors with positive beliefs. Forgive yourself when you make mistakes. Remember that you are perfectly worthy. Affirm yourself by recalling positive experiences and envisioning the life you dream. Remember that you're not a bad person just because you may be in a bad situation. If you haven't practiced this approach in the past, start today with one of the suggestions above.

Only when you are accepting of yourself can you become accepting of others. Don't fool yourself into believing that you can be nasty to yourself and loving to other people. You can't. Charity begins at home. The deepest and most profound love is unconditional. Grow unconditional love within yourself and you will be able to give it away, too.

53.
Protect your relationships.

Unless you live in total isolation, other people are vital to the quality of your life. Relationships enhance your success and your happiness. If you're not protecting relationships with your spouse and children, then you're not going to have a decent family life. If you're not protecting relationships with customers, then you're not going to be selling many products or services. If you're not protecting relationships with co-workers, direct reports and bosses, then you're not going to be very effective at work.

The kind of interactions you have with family, friends, co-workers, customers, etc., is a reflection of how strongly you value the relationship. When you truly value your connections with others, you are willing to put the relationship first – to protect it. If the relationship hits a bump in the road, then you put other tasks on "hold" until you get the relationship back on track again. When you protect relationships in this way, you keep them high on your priority list, and you demonstrate that belief to others through your behaviors.

When we realize that all of our daily tasks are not separate from our relationships, then we see how success in one area can breed success in another. Relationships are the critical element that connect everything. If you want to get more sales, be a better manager, ship the goods on time, build a strong company or be more effective at work or at home, take a good look at your relationships. Better relationships yield better results everywhere.

54.
Address little hurts before they become big hurts.

The first reason for this mindset is to keep little things from stacking up and becoming overwhelming due to sheer volume. Get those little things off your shoulders as fast as you can because there are going to be some new ones coming in the future, and they can become too emotionally heavy for you to carry them all at one time.

Besides stacking up, little hurts will grow out of proportion over time. Did you ever notice that the longer an issue goes unresolved, the more upset you can become? When hurts are exaggerated they become tougher to resolve.

Address little hurts before they become big hurts. You'll have more energy for your positive and healthy encounters. You'll have more opportunity to forgive and truly forget. You'll maintain more loving relationships and carry less emotional burden.

55.
When you most want to retreat, stay engaged.

This concept doesn't apply to someone who's being beaten or abused in any way. It is about the everyday misconnects with people who are important to you. They may say things that hurt you and make you want to withdraw. When you start to think, "I'm out of here," and then turn and walk away, you have physically and figuratively "done a 180." A better alternative, however, is to stop and talk it out before anyone walks away. It requires that you talk about how you're feeling, listen to the other person and do whatever you can to protect the relationship. (See Number 53.)

Some people stay in the vicinity but still do emotional 180s. These are the behaviors that are exactly the opposite (180 degrees) from what the person desires as an outcome. When people do emotional 180s, they send signals that something is wrong and then expect others to guess what is the matter. They may say they don't want to talk about a problem when they really do want to talk. They may say they don't care when, in fact, they care very much. They may say they don't want to know when they do want to know. They may slam cupboard doors, sigh heavily or mutter under their breath. Even when others approach them and ask what is wrong, the response may well be, "Nothing!" When they say nothing is wrong, you can be pretty sure that something is wrong.

If you have the tendency to engage in 180-degree behaviors, it will take a different mindset to stay engaged and keep talking when you're hurt or you feel like you've been "done wrong." You can't expect others to read your mind. It's helpful to tell the other person that you're fighting off the temptation to disengage, but you're choosing instead to stay. The other individual has a responsibility to do the same thing. If you turn and walk away, chances are good that you'll be away for quite some time. But if you stay engaged, you'll be able to resolve small misunderstandings while they're still the size of molehills. In order to protect relationships, it is important to resist the temptation to do a 180. Stay engaged when you want to retreat.

56.
Be sure you know why you're apologizing.

The real value of an apology is in the depth of understanding that we've hurt someone else and in the depth of our desire to make amends.

Have you ever found yourself apologizing when you weren't sure what you had done, but you knew you had provoked someone's wrath? Or have you ever given someone a gift or "peace offering" because it was actually easier to do that than to talk about the issue? These deeds may soothe the issue, but they won't resolve it.

The fact is, inadvertently or not, you've hurt someone else. They need to hear that you understand WHY that particular transgression was hurtful and that you are truly sorry. (Helpful hint: If you don't have a clue what is wrong, ask them!) Then they can be reasonably confident that you will not repeat it inadvertently. In the beginning, they may not even know the real reason they're upset. For example, if you borrow your sister's vehicle and return it with an empty gas tank and litter on the seats, she may be upset about the condition of the vehicle. However, after some discussion, you may both realize that she is not hurt about how you treated the vehicle, per se. The real hurt is in her perception that, if you don't respect her vehicle, you don't respect *her*. (See Number 45.) As painful as it is, the communication has to take place in order to identify and resolve the real hurt.

When you say "I'm sorry" and really mean it, the connection, the reconnection, with the other person will actually strengthen your relationship. Conversely, if you don't resolve the issue right now, it will surely come back later as part of a bigger package.

57.
Try to turn your hurt and anger into understanding and compassion.

From time to time, you may find reason to play a "somebody done somebody wrong" song. Something happens that is hurtful to you. After a while, the hurt fades and you become angry. That anger can grow and become like a festering wound. You mentally revisit the incident over and over again. No matter how many times you "replay the tape," your hurt and anger continue to haunt you.

If you find yourself in this situation, make it a mission to analyze the motivation behind other people's actions. What is their frame of reference? What fears might cause them to mistreat you? How might they describe the incident? Try to give them the benefit of the doubt. Did they deliberately kick you (figuratively), or did they just stumble over you? Did they do the best they could, even though they may not have had the best methods? Could it be that they were truly well intentioned?

When you analyze in this way, you will usually come up with some insights that allow you to soften your position. The better you understand the opposing position, the less embedded you remain in yours. Your focus then changes from "who was right?" to "how can we get past this?" It leads to understanding, and understanding leads to compassion.

58.
Ask people: "Do you know what I like about you?"

It's quite simple to ask someone, "Do you know what I like about you?" This question allows you to supply the answer yourself. Maybe you want to comment on something obvious like, "I'm glad you always pick up after yourself" or "I appreciate that you keep your work area neat" or "You have a pleasant disposition." More importantly, however, you have the opportunity to comment on something deeper – like the individual's personal culture or character. For example, when a dad asks his daughter, "Do you know what I like about you?" he can respond with answers like: "I really like that you treat other people with dignity" or "I really like that you kept talking to me today even though you were angry and wanted to walk away" or "I really like your determination and optimism."

After a few weeks of these exchanges, you will build a routine that is especially valuable with family members. They may start to supply their own answers, or guess what your answer will be. But they can be assured that you'll have something good to say, even if they have hurt your feelings or damaged your vehicle or dropped out of school. In the closest relationships, you can conclude your responses with a promise: "I'll always love you no matter what." Now they know that you love them, even when you're angry or hurt or disappointed.

When you tell others what you like about them, or what you love about them, you are teaching them to love themselves. When you hold them in high esteem, you are teaching them to value themselves. When you pass on unconditional love, you are helping them to become how they really want to be. This is one of the most powerful things you can ever do for another person.

59.
Look for relationships with synergy.

The best relationships provide a love, acceptance and energy which exceeds that of each individual. Synergy occurs when people with strong personal cultures come together to form a union – a new single entity – with a shared interpersonal culture that encourages them both to be how they want to be. It strengthens them as individuals and as partners. In synergistic relationships, people bring out the best in each other. They accept themselves and each other unconditionally. They serve as catalysts for each other, helping each other become even better, yet taking responsibility for their own self-improvement. They champion each other. They support each other. Yet they are not dependent upon each other. The best relationships form when two or more individuals join in the common pursuit of dreams and goals, even though they are personally centered and strong alone. In short, the most synergistic relationships are mergers, not acquisitions.

In these relationships, people aren't looking for anyone else to make them "whole" or to "complete" them. They aren't looking for anyone to fill in their gaps or shore up their weaknesses. They don't just average out each other. If, for example, you think you're a good match because one of you is high strung and the other is very laid back, you may want to take a closer look. Long-term happiness is not found in partners who "balance out" or "neutralize" us. The result of such relationships is mediocrity for both partners. Even worse, dysfunctional relationships are easily created when one partner tries to "fix" the other one, or when both partners aren't committed to the union.

The best relationships are truly complementary. These relationships strengthen and enhance our personal cultures, which help us build a powerful interpersonal culture. We feel like we're better individuals because the partnership is so good. We want to become even better individuals because the union is already strong. Ironically, the synergistic partnerships that strengthen us as individuals will also inspire us to become even better partners.

60.
Don't take love for granted.

There is no status quo with love. Relationships never stay where you left them. If you're not doing something to improve them, they are going to diminish by default. It's like pushing a car up a hill; as soon as you stop pushing, it's going to start rolling backwards.

Suppose you filled ice cube trays with water and placed them in the freezer. If you leave them unattended too long, you will eventually notice that the ice cubes are getting smaller – they are evaporating. Even something as hard as ice, or a relationship as solid as ice, can deteriorate or evaporate if you're not adding to it and tending to it. The mindset is: If you're not adding something to a relationship all the time, it too will begin to evaporate.

Loving relationships need to be nurtured and guarded and rejuvenated. They need your time and attention, just like a small child or a new business. If you don't continually invest yourself, you won't reap many rewards, and you may wake up one day and find that you're alone.

Don't take love for granted. It's a rare and special thing. When your life is graced with it, acknowledge that, cherish it and work hard to keep it a priority. If you don't view it as one of your mountains, it's likely to become a molehill that's lost in the shuffle.

61.
Spend some time each evening getting "settled in" with your family.

When family members have gone their separate ways all day, it's important to emotionally converge when you all physically return to the same house in the evening. This is the process of coming together again, mentally and emotionally, and reconnecting with each other.

A good tool for settling in is to spend the first 15 minutes giving each other undivided attention. Don't come home and rush into the kitchen or the garage. Instead, spend a few uninterrupted minutes with each other. Look at each other and really listen. Get the summary of everyone's day and establish a plan for the evening. If someone has a pressing issue to discuss, they will know that they have your full attention. This is much more effective than trying to interrupt someone else's activities in the evening. After some minutes together, people are generally ready to return to their tasks, but they will have a calmer demeanor. By spending some time on this converging process, you make a strong statement that your relationships are more important than things like the football game or the Internet or the lawn or the mail.

It may be appropriate for you to repeat the converging process again, before bedtime. This is a good opportunity to transition between high activity levels and rest. Your routine could include reading stories to small children, saying special prayers, giving hugs and kisses, sharing a cup of coffee or cuddling on the couch. It helps you to disconnect with daily issues and turn your focus to loved ones in a peaceful, quiet, close way. You'll feel affirmed and more content, and so will your family.

62.
Share food.

Sharing food is sharing love. There is immense symbolism associated with sharing food. Think of all the times you have offered (or received) fruitcakes, casseroles, cheese, sausage, bread, soup and cookies. When we offer something from our kitchen or plate, we show someone that we cherish them.

Additionally, we often celebrate with food. Birthday parties, weddings, reunions and other notable occasions usually involve a lot of food. When we eat together, we typically talk, listen and laugh together. While nourishing our bodies, we also nourish our souls with the familiar clinking sounds of utensils, the enticing aroma of food being prepared and the comforting camaraderie of family.

Sharing food is showing affection. It's believing that there's always enough for all of us. It's wanting to see your loved ones enjoy some of your food more than you want to enjoy it yourself. It's giving of yourself, and receiving for yourself at the same time.

63.
Build memories of
special moments.

Many of the best memories are made in moments, not events. When people tell and retell stories of special memories, they talk about a silly comment or a practical joke or a spontaneous situation. The focus isn't on the holiday or the occasion (although that may be mentioned for reference); it's on the moments of special and memorable fun.

Big events are fine. But don't overlook the special moments within them and between them. When we focus too far into the future, we lose the opportunity to experience joy in the present. (See Number 81.) When we exaggerate the importance of an event, we're likely to find that our great expectations exceed what any event could provide and we're left disappointed when the event has passed.

The sweetest moments are comfortable, relaxed, spontaneous and emotionally rich. These moments will one day become our most precious memories.

PARENTING
AND
FAMILY

64.
Let your children see that you're not perfect.

Parents who try to be too perfect or won't admit mistakes may be setting up their children for a lot of disappointment. Perfection is a standard that parents cannot meet. While we want to do our best for our children, we do them a disservice if they grow up thinking that, one day, they will have to be perfect parents for their children.

"Perfect parents" build barriers. It's tough for children to relate to people who seem never to lose, forget, worry, hurt, fail, or apologize. Additionally, when children idolize their parents and then see them fall from the pedestal, it can be very difficult to accept that their parents are, in fact, mere mortals. "Imperfect parents," however, are more approachable and lovable. It's easier to build a relationship with parents who show a full range of emotions and admit mistakes. It's a learning experience when children see their parents struggle with an issue, work through it and resolve it. It enhances a child's self-image when a parent says "I'm sorry" to a child. Big people aren't always right. And little people aren't always wrong. Even when we're not perfect, we can still be perfectly worthy. This belief may well be the best thing we can attain for ourselves. And it's the best thing we can help our children attain for themselves.

Children learn more about the process of becoming a good big person (that is, growing up) when they see it realistically portrayed. When we don't hold ourselves or anyone else to unattainable standards, we can learn from each other. We can show our children that we accept ourselves even when we make mistakes. We can also encourage them to practice that same acceptance of themselves.

65.
Help little people grow up to be good big people.

The primary job of a parent is to help little people grow up to be good big people. A simple analogy is a mama bird that cares for her babies when they are tiny and nudges them to the edge of the nest when they are ready to fly. A helpful mindset for parents is: What can I do today to prepare my children for the future?

Babies need intense care from parents. But as children mature, they need to learn how to care for themselves. For example, parents can get their children ready for school by telling them to get dressed, eat a good breakfast, brush their teeth, comb their hair and to hurry up with it all. Or, parents can teach their children that they need to be ready for school by 8 a.m. The latter approach requires that children take responsibility for being ready on time, instead of the parents owning that responsibility.

Here's the theory behind the practice: Think about how old your children will be when you would expect them to be "totally independent." You may guess, for example, that it would be somewhere between ages 18 and 25. This means that when they're seven or eight, they're about one-third of the way to full independence. (Keep in mind that the line is curved on this figurative maturity scale. Children may need to be more than one-third of the age of full maturity before they are actually one-third independent.) The idea is to keep an eye on the maturity curve and continually assess if you're gently nudging children up the scale in ways that are appropriate for their age or if, instead, you're holding them back.

The objective is to stay focused on teaching your children how to take care of themselves, rather than getting too preoccupied with giving care to them. While it's a blessing to have small babies in your nest, the time will come when they want to fly. With these mindsets and tools, you can have confidence that you're preparing them to be good big people as they prepare to strike out on their own.

66.
Instill in children a sense of conviction, courage and character (the three Cs).

It's important to seek a balance in the kinds of knowledge we share with our children. We may naturally impart knowledge about subjects like reading, writing and arithmetic (with much help, of course, from the school systems). It is equally important, however, to instill knowledge in children about themselves – their convictions, courage and character. There needs to be a balance of these three Cs (and other related principles) with the more typical three Rs (and other school subjects).

It's not too difficult to instill the three Cs. In fact, our own actions may teach them quite well. For example, when children watch their parents willingly pay the appropriate admission rates for a matinee movie (even though the children could have passed for younger ages and cheaper prices), the children observe character in action. When children hear their parents say they are afraid to learn new things (like programming the VCR) and then children watch their parents learn how to do it anyway, the children learn that everyone has courage even if they are afraid. When children see parents volunteer time and talent for church or school activities, children learn about the strength of convictions.

We instill a sense of character, courage and conviction each time we tell our children about these traits and each time our children observe our embodiment of the traits. Additionally, when our children try to emulate our three Cs, we can compliment their behaviors and encourage them to continue. This kind of personal development will enhance our children's intellectual development, providing a good balance for them to draw upon in future endeavors.

67.
Teach your children to behave in ways that are responsible, respectful, reliable and trustworthy (RRRT).

R RRT is a valuable tool for defining expected behaviors. Instead of telling children all the things that are off limits and what they should not do, parents can use RRRT to help teach children HOW TO BE so children can decide for themselves what they should do. If children consistently follow these guidelines, their actions will usually be on target. If, for example, a child has to make a decision, and there's no one else to ask for guidance, he or she can run through the list: "If I do this, am I being Responsible, am I being Respectful, am I being Reliable, am I being Trustworthy?" If the action passes all these tests, it's probably an okay thing to do.

When parents adopt the RRRT tool, they free themselves from continually saying "no" and, instead, define acceptable behaviors. When children learn RRRT, they give up the trial-and-error approach to decision making and, instead, understand exactly what is expected. When everyone in the family knows that RRRT are the guiding principles for behavior, the detail decisions come easy.

68.
Ask a grandparent or other older relative to tell you about your roots.

This is your connection to your extended family, your ancestors and your heritage. It helps you understand where you come from and how you fit into a bigger picture.

To learn about your history is to prepare for the future. You start to see the whole range of multiple generations. You see the context of past, present and future. You become aware of where your family has been, where you are now, and where you are going. When grandparents tell stories, you learn of a life you never experienced. You may realize, for example, that many parents of Baby Boomers didn't have indoor plumbing or electric lights when they were youngsters. Now imagine what life was like for their parents! It puts a much different perspective on our computer games, microwave ovens and e-mail. It helps you more fully appreciate what you have and what you can offer to those who will come after you.

If you want to enrich your grandparents' lives (and your own), ask them to talk about their memories. Watch them pull grandchildren onto their laps and paint vivid pictures in the children's innocent eyes. You will value your roots. You'll enjoy the present moment. And you'll look forward to someday telling stories of your own.

69.
When you leave an item for someone to inherit, leave a short, handwritten note explaining why the item is special.

It's common practice to save "treasures" for people to inherit. The sad part is, that frequently, those things are meaningless unless the recipient understands the sentimental value associated with them. This is why one person's treasure can so easily become another person's trash.

When a handwritten note accompanies the item, there are typically stories or memories or feelings explained about the item. (And a handwritten note provides a much more personal connection than something prepared electronically.) Then the recipient can understand why the item is important and why it was saved. The recipient may better appreciate the item. But often it's not the item itself that really becomes cherished. It is the stories and memories and feelings that are triggered by the item and supplied in the NOTE.

Inherited items are most cherished when they symbolize something special about your relationship with another person. Whether or not the item is of substantial material value, the feelings are valued strongly. The "trinkets" may come and go, but the feelings endure. The note conveys the feelings, which is why the note may become far more important than any "thing" left behind. Additionally, as you write these notes, you will have the pleasure of knowing that future generations will learn how you touched other people's lives, and that your memory will live on.

ON THE JOB

70.
Don't confuse happiness with success.

A chieving success and attaining happiness are parallel pursuits. They are not mutually inclusive. You can pursue them at the same time, but independently of each other.

Don't make the mistake of thinking that when you have attained a certain job, position or title, you're sure to be happy. Don't bide your time thinking everything will be better when you're making more money or when you have more influence in the company. You can look for happiness right now, regardless of your job status. You can be successful, and you can be happy. Just remember that job success doesn't guarantee happiness.

71.
Remember that high salaries steal freedom.

It has been said that you can have anything you want as long as you're willing to pay the price. Ironically, that adage applies to income levels, too. Money may buy freedom, but high salaries can bear some high personal prices.

Salaries are usually proportionate with job responsibilities and demands. While you may wish to earn more money, are you also ready to take on the additional workload that goes with the additional income? Do you want to have more stress, responsibility and travel? Are you willing to work longer hours and be away from your family for longer periods of time? Are you willing to put the additional "head time" into the position, even when you're not at work? In short, are you willing to make a higher level of personal investment in order to earn a higher salary?

You may find the additional stress and workload to be a fair trade with the corresponding increases in salary and authority. Or you may find that handcuffs are always handcuffs, even if they're made of gold. Whatever path you choose, do your homework first, so you can determine your preferred balance of income and freedom.

72.
Use a balance of logic and emotion to find the best job for you.

Statistics show that adults change jobs, and even occupations, several times during their work life. When you're facing a job change, it can be difficult to know which position to pursue because there are so many factors in the decision. To clear your thinking, it may be helpful to remember that there are two major issues at hand: Questions of logic and questions of emotion.

Emotional concerns may include: Do I have a real interest in this kind of work? How long might I enjoy doing this kind of job? Do I like to have a clearly defined role, or do I prefer more flexibility? Do I like to work autonomously, or do I prefer to work in groups and teams? How important are flexibility and independence? Am I choosing this job because it's right for me, or am I being pressured by family members or others to take this job?

Logical questions may include: Where is the job located? Is there a reasonable amount of job security? What income can I expect? What are the opportunities for promotion or lateral moves? What are the working conditions? Do I meet the qualifications?*

When you separate your questions into these two categories, it becomes much easier to determine which factors are of critical importance. When you've looked at both sides of the coin and balanced logic and emotion, you'll have more confidence that you've made the best decision with the information you had.

While the lists above are only intended to gain a general idea, and not to be all inclusive, they do give a flavor of the types of questions you may wish to generate.

73.
Decide if you want the job or the position.

This may sound like a question of semantics, but the job and the position are actually two very separate issues. A job is the work you do – the actual tasks and responsibilities that you typically find written in a job description. A position, on the other hand, includes the perks you receive – like the title, office location and size, parking space, salary, etc. Especially when you're being recruited, people will want to talk with you about all the perks you could expect from a position. While such things are very appealing, be sure to keep a clear focus on the job duties and responsibilities. A job may bring you many perks. But perks will never make the work of the job more fun or meaningful.

Take, for example, a salesperson who has been offered a promotion to sales management. The new position may include a title of vice president or manager, more money, a nicer office, more vacation, etc. The duties of the job, however, are not just "upgraded" sales work. The scope of the job changes significantly to include supervision of direct reports, budgeting, sales forecasting, performance evaluations, etc. It's important, then to ask yourself, "Do I want the work of the job or do I want the perks of the position?"

While new perks are nice at first, they are quickly lost in the shuffle, and then all that's left is the work. If you are eager to do the work involved, go for it. But if you honestly decide that the work isn't appealing, deliberate carefully about taking that job. A "good" position is seldom enough to compensate for a "bad" job.

74.
Focus more on your job
than on your career.

Try not to worry too much about climbing the corporate ladder, per se. Concentrate, instead, on doing a good job and meeting or exceeding the expectations of your customers.

Look for the intrinsic value in your work. You will reap pride and pleasure from doing meaningful work. But if you're simply looking for a promotion or a way to look good politically, your co-workers will quickly sense your real motives. That causes working relationships to suffer, and you'll find it difficult to accomplish goals alone.

Focus on the job. Go to work with an attitude of, "How can I contribute?" instead of "What can I collect?" This approach is usually more ingratiating to people in higher levels of authority. Teamwork and participation can earn you more recognition and rewards than being the lone superstar. When you stay focused on doing good work, your career will take care of itself.

75.
When you've got a big job ahead of you, the first thing to do is GET ORGANIZED.

When projects, assignments or even simple tasks seem overwhelming or chaotic, the tool of "getting organized" helps you get back on top of the issues and take control again. Before diving into the details, take some time to step back and review the whole situation. What is the scope? What is the strategy? What are all the issues? What has to be done? What is the time frame? How much will it cost? What am I trying to accomplish? The tool of getting organized applies to a whole range of work, from sorting through your mail to generating detailed project plans.

Invest some time up front. Instead of forging ahead immediately, take a good look at the issue from an overall perspective. Picture the final outcome in your mind and plan accordingly. When you begin the actual work, things will come together much more quickly and with fewer false starts or false steps. The time invested in getting organized will pay large dividends both in total time required and in total effort expended.

76.
Drive the first nail.

A ssume you're starting a big project. Once you're organized your next challenge is to take action. When you move from planning to doing, it's common to feel a reluctance about taking the first step. In fact, you're likely to experience "cold feet syndrome"– the feeling that it seemed like a good idea some time ago when you committed to the project, but now that it's time to deliver, things seem pretty scary.

Instead of rationalizing why you should delay the project or why you really need more prep time, decide only to drive the first nail. This psychological tool helps you commit to taking action – one small step – without committing to completing the whole project right now. It makes the first task look easy. Anyone can envision driving a single nail, even when the rest of the project seems daunting.

This simple technique gets you over the initial hurdle and into the meat of the project. Odds are pretty good that, once you drive the first nail, you'll keep pounding until you've made good progress.

77.
Use simple,
straight-forward language.

Have you ever sat in a business meeting listening to people talking in a way that sounded so high level that you didn't have a clue what they were saying? There seems to be almost an epidemic of high-brow jargon related to quality, psychology and technology. All the buzzwords and acronyms can start to sound like a foreign language, and you feel like a foreigner. If you don't understand what's being said, odds are that others in the audience don't understand it either. What a sad situation. We seem to have forgotten that it's the speaker's responsibility to use words that can be understood.

When you're the speaker, don't use lofty terms or try to impress people. They won't be impressed. Use plain, simple words. The fewer syllables the better. Give people a chance to understand you. When your message is clear and crisp, people will understand you. And incidentally, they also will be impressed!

78.
When receiving feedback,
be like a reporter.

It's quite easy to receive positive feedback. But the challenge comes when you're hearing anything less than totally positive comments. It's best to try to set emotion aside for a while and focus on the facts. Figuratively, put on a reporter's hat and think of yourself as a third person. Distance yourself emotionally while you send the "reporter" to collect the comments. Don't worry, you'll have plenty of time to personally sort it all out later.

A reporter's job is to get information: who, what, where, when, why and how. Reporters don't express opinions unless they write editorials, which serve a totally different purpose. Your reporter persona will collect information without passing judgment, jumping to conclusions or expressing rebuttals – typical responses that prevent emotionally involved people from hearing an accurate message. The reporter will listen openly, ask for examples, ask clarifying questions and take good notes.

Later on, you can remove your reporter's hat and review the notes. You can look at the information more objectively. You can sift, sort and replay the comments until you have absorbed them completely. Then you are in a position to decide what you will accept, what you will reject and what you may want to change. Your evaluation process will be more valuable and you will have a better understanding of the information because your "reporter" will have provided some emotional armor. As a result, you may glean useful feedback to help you become more effective. You take the responsibility for any necessary changes in your work and for the final evaluation of your work. It's a much better alternative to sitting through an uncomfortable review process only to decide, in the end, that the process is worthless and your boss is clueless.

79.
Be aware of the
"I Quit Dip."

Even dreams-come-true can seem like nightmares after you've lived them for a while. Suppose you finally landed a job with a company you've always wanted to work for. Or maybe you just got promoted and can now start working on the projects you've coveted. Or maybe you have finally taken the leap into entrepreneurship and started your own business. At first, you're likely to feel very excited and optimistic. You can't wait to dive in and start doing all the things you've eagerly anticipated. People are congratulating you and encouraging you. You feel confident because, after all, these things wouldn't be happening if you weren't worthy of the additional responsibilities or authority.

Shortly after you've gotten into the new routine, however, the "I Quit Dip" sets in. The perks of the new position have faded, and now you're left with challenging work, hard questions (because you don't know the answers yet) and bigger demands than you've ever had. It feels like chaos, and you're not sure if you're on foot or horseback. The "I Quit Dip" hits you like a punch in the ribs, and it haunts you with a vengeance: Why did I ever think I wanted to do this? What have I done? Maybe I'm in over my head. You know you've hit the bottom of the "I Quit Dip" when you're thinking, "Maybe I should get out of here."

Whenever you make a major change in your job (or any other aspect of your life), you're likely to find that, after a short time, your excitement and confidence will give way to disillusionment and uncertainty. This dip is a very predictable step in the process. However, you can rest assured that, after a brief period in the dip, you will recover. You'll find that the tasks and your emotions reach a normal state of equilibrium again. Your confidence returns and you start to think that this is going to be okay after all. Recognize that the "I Quit Dip" is a temporary situation, and take heart. Many others have survived this, and you will too.

80.
Don't write off ANYONE.

Everyone deserves respect for who they are, regardless of the position they hold or the circumstances of the moment. For example, if someone has been demoted, fired or fallen out of favor, it's still judicious to acknowledge them and treat them with respect. It may be tempting to make wisecracks or to flaunt their loss of position or power. However, your ability to resist those temptations is an indicator of your personal culture and character. Under difficult circumstances, the deference you show others is a bigger reflection on you than it is on them.

There's another aspect to this concept, too. You never know when you're going to encounter the same person in the future, or what the circumstances will be at that time. Perhaps the roles will be reversed! If you were respectful of them in the past, you won't have to worry about what you've said or how you've behaved. Be respectful of other people, regardless of their status.

EVERYDAY
LIFE

81.
Experience joy every day.

There is a potential for joy within each of us that we can choose to experience or we can choose to ignore. If you want to keep a more joyful presence, make it a priority to look for joy and share it with others.

Joyful people typically have three things in common: They anticipate, they participate and they appreciate. Suppose a group of people are planning a fishing trip. They're likely to anticipate the trip and prepare for it six months in advance. They'll plan where to go, how to get there and which gear to take. They may study maps and develop strategies to ensure they're fishing where the fish are likely to be biting. They'll probably check their equipment, or purchase more, so they're sure to have everything they might need.

After all this anticipation, they'll actually take the trip. They'll participate in the event for maybe six days. They will enjoy the humorous moments and the excitement. They'll notice nature. They'll laugh together. They may even catch a few fish. And then, for maybe as long as six years, they'll appreciate the trip. They'll tell stories about "the big one that got away" or how clever they were to catch fish of "good eating size." Little memory triggers in the future will cause them to recall the trip, and to share stories again and again.

The joys are found in getting ready (anticipation), doing (participation), and then reliving the experience (appreciation). This three-step process is what converts endearing moments into enduring joy.

Joy is worth more to you right now than it will ever be in the future. You can't save it or invest it. You can't will it to your children. So indulge in joy each day.

82.
Be silly; laugh out loud.

This is a simple way to put a little more life into every day. It's fun to have fun. It's also good for all the people around you to see you laughing out loud and, perhaps, to laugh with you. It adds levity and value to everyday experiences.

Appropriate silliness and laughter help us feel less burdened and improve our physical demeanor. Picture people who are in the midst of a good belly laugh. They're leaning back with an open posture. They may have tears rolling down their cheeks, yet you know they're having a positive experience. Their breathing is deep and relaxed. They are approachable; in fact, it's tempting to join in the laughter and find out what was so funny. They are experiencing joy, and as a result, they are having a rich experience.

To laugh and be silly is good for you and those around you. It's good for your emotions, your body and your soul. And it's self-perpetuating because it creates an environment that encourages more spontaneous laughter in the future.

83.
Remember that a person in a bad situation is not necessarily a bad person.

A cartoon about Rudolph the Red-Nosed Reindeer depicts a number of toys that have fallen into misfortune. Trains may have square wheels and jack-in-the-boxes may be named Charlie. These toys are banished to the Island of Misfit Toys because it is believed that, due to some nonconformity, they cannot be accepted and loved by children. The toys didn't fit some assumed standards and accepted practices, so they were considered bad – misfits. Under different circumstances, the same toys may have fit well on the shelves of F.A.O. Schwartz, looking all shiny and new. The situation may change, but the toys are the same. So it is with us. Different circumstances can determine whether we're perceived as a good fit or a misfit, even though we haven't changed at all.

When the culture of a family, an organization or a relationship changes around you, it's very possible to find yourself in a bad situation. That doesn't make you a bad person. When unforeseen events put you at a disadvantage, that doesn't mean you are disadvantaged. It may be tempting to think that if something bad happens to us, we must be bad people. We may think, for some reason, we don't deserve anything better. We may think that if only we were better or perfect, we never would have had that car accident, gotten divorced, failed the test, lost the job, been "passed over" for the promotion, yelled at the kids, had a child who dropped out of school, etc.

Remember that circumstances change overnight; people don't. If you're in a bad situation, take action to change your perspective, change the situation, or get away from it. But don't beat yourself up in the meantime. And don't be too hard on others who may be temporarily visiting the Island of Misfit Toys.

84.
Fears are nested. Ask yourself "why" several times to get to the root of a fear.

Have you ever seen a set of nested objects, like egg-shaped Russian dolls? Each doll opens in half and holds the next smaller doll. All together, the dolls may range in size from about an inch to about a foot, with the smallest one being very well hidden inside all the others. Fears are nested inside of each other just like those dolls. The smallest fear may be unseen and therefore difficult to identify.

To get to the root of your fears, go through the exercise of asking "why" several times. For example, you may dread the idea of giving a speech or making a presentation. Why? Because it's scary to stand up in front of people and talk. Why? Because there's so much to remember, like how to stand and which visual aids to use, and how to express your main point. Why is that scary? Because you may not do it all as well as you would like. Why? Because you're pretty sure you'll make a mistake and other people will laugh and you'll be embarrassed. Why? Because this would show you're not perfect. In this scenario, then, you may think the fear is about public speaking, but the REAL fear may be about imperfection or embarrassment. When a hidden fear is identified, you can go about overcoming it. (See Number 85.)

A root fear can haunt us in numerous ways. The fear of being imperfect may hide itself in a casing that looks like fear of public speaking. But it may also disguise itself in casings that look like fear of making decisions, fear of success, fear of failure, fear of change, etc. That small fear can become multiplied and disproportionately large until you deal with it. When you overcome one small nested fear, you may conquer several bigger ones.

85.
Overcome fear through identification, information and action.

F ears can be terrifying, overwhelming and paralyzing UNTIL we identify the root fear, get information and take action.

To identify a fear, ask "why" several times until you reveal a hidden fear and understand it. (See Number 84.) Then learn about what scares you and why it scares you. Get factual information and details (who, what, when, where, etc.). Quantify things whenever possible. The more you know, the less you fear.

As you gain knowledge, you prepare yourself to take action – to move from hand wringing to doing something that moves you one small step forward and one large step away from the fear. If, for example, you fear public speaking, you may find the real fear to be that you won't make a perfect presentation. Now you're in a position to educate yourself about public speaking and to gather information on how the professionals do it. Then you can take action by organizing your notes, preparing your visual materials and rehearsing in front of a mirror or video camera. As part of this planning process, consider all your "what if" questions. For example, what if, during the presentation, the overhead projector bulb burns out? As part of your preparation you can check where the spare bulb is, learn how to switch the bulbs and test the spare to make sure it's still useable.

When you've identified and mastered your "what if" fears, they dissipate almost immediately. These three tools – identification, information and action – make it possible for you to imagine how good it will be to get past the fear. Then you can summon the courage to meet it head-on.

We all have fears. We are all challenged daily to overcome our fears. The question is whether we'll let them intimidate us out of living as we would like to live, or if we'll acknowledge them and move on in spite of them. When you identify fears, get information and take action, you take back the power you would otherwise relinquish to insidious fear.

86.
Recognize that intimidating behavior is driven by fear.

A dults who practice intimidating behaviors are often much like the bullies of your grade-school days. They may taunt you or pressure you into the behavior they want. They may be sarcastic. They may criticize you. They may lead you to believe that they have power and information you don't. They may actively throw temper tantrums or passively pout in order to manipulate you. They may flaunt their experience, knowledge, possessions, connections, or rank – especially if they have more than you.

These people may be masters of intimidation, but you can develop the mindset that you will not be a victim. Once you decide that you won't be needlessly bullied, they can't bully you anymore.

Fear drives most intimidating behavior. And fear drives most cowardly behavior. If you operate within the parameters of a strong personal culture, you will find the courage to take the high road and respectfully stand up to intimidators. Ironically, as soon as you change your behavior, they are likely to change theirs. When you no longer view yourself as their victim, they'll probably stop treating you like one. If you can convert your hurt and anger into understanding and compassion, you may even be able to forgive them.

Treat people, including yourself, with the respect and dignity they deserve. Especially in the presence of bullies, try to keep your focus on being how you really want to be. Choose a quietly confident demeanor with appropriate actions, and you will no longer be driven by the fear of others.

87.
Don't expect logic to overcome emotion.

Human beings have a huge capacity to process information and a huge capacity to feel emotions. Although the two are very separate, we frequently try to overlap them and use logic to overcome emotions. The result is typically a long list of logical reasons which support your position or indicate that everything is okay; yet a nagging feeling still persists, telling you that something isn't right.

How often do we try to talk ourselves into or out of feeling something by using information, data or statistics? It doesn't work. You cannot use logic to overcome unexposed emotions. Instead, try using this tool when you're struggling with a tough issue: Make a list with three columns labeled WHAT I KNOW, WHAT I WANT and WHAT I FEAR. Then complete the lists as your thoughts pertain. You will usually find that the WANT and FEAR lists are emotion driven, while the KNOW list is more logical and factual. Having separated the emotional issues from the logical thoughts, it's best to deal with the emotions first. Allow yourself time to sort out what you're feeling. It will take less time than you think. After those issues are resolved, you can move easily to the logical issues and make good use of your data and statistics.

When you address your emotions and then incorporate logic, you will be comfortable with your decisions, and you will proceed with confidence.

88.
If you're overwhelmed
or can't resolve something
in your mind, it's probably
because a number of issues
are "stacking up."

Have you ever seen the sky so full of ducks that you couldn't identify one from another? It can be difficult to get a good focus on one duck when there are so many. And it can seem like chaos when they're all moving. Now picture a shooting gallery with metal models of those ducks lined up, one after another. It's quite easy to identify them and deal with them because the chaos is gone and your view is clear.

The same concept applies to fears or other problems in our lives. When you're overreacting to small things or feeling overwhelmed, it pays to look back at what has occurred in the last several days. It's likely that several issues have stacked up. Maybe the car broke down, the project is behind schedule, the children are sick, and you've gained weight, etc. Start, first, by figuratively lining your ducks up in the shooting gallery.

Make a list of all the issues. Identify their importance and urgency so that you can prioritize them. Then develop an action plan consisting of one or two things you can do to address each issue.

By identifying the issues and determining the plan, you take appropriate actions to get the situation under control and to regain your perspective. Then, you're prepared to take aim and address each issue with confidence. Next time you feel like there are ducks flying everywhere, try to picture yourself lining them up so you can identify them and deal with them. Take them one at a time, and you'll be fine.

89.
Remember that very few decisions in life are irrevocable.

The decisions a college freshman makes at the beginning of a semester will seem to be major decisions at that time. Which college is the best choice? Where to live? What classes to take? Which major to declare? But in reality, these decisions will only last for one semester, or maybe even less.

We make many, many big decisions in our lives. But very few of our choices cannot be changed. Remembering that few decisions are irrevocable is a tool for keeping decisions in perspective. If you find that you're not at peace with your decisions about where you go to school, which job you take or where you live, etc., you can change your mind. If your initial choices don't work out, there are probably other options available. You just need to stay flexible and open to alternatives.

When you're facing what seems to be a big decision, ask yourself, "How long will I have to live with this decision? And what's the worst thing that can happen?" If you'll have to face the consequences for a long time, or if the consequences could be severe, then give the decision substantial consideration. But, if you realize the decision lasts a very limited time, then the big decision becomes much smaller – and you lighten your burden mentally and emotionally. You have more confidence to make the decision, and new-found flexibility to change your mind. Every decision is not a "mountain" decision. Work hard to keep "molehill" decisions in perspective.

90.
Always "sleep on" a major decision for at least one night.

Major decisions connotate long-term implications. And long-term issues rarely require that you make immediate or urgent decisions. With issues like this, it's dangerous to make quick decisions because you may well repent at leisure, or at least live with the negative ramifications for a long time.

There's a better option. You can almost always let a major decision wait for 24 hours minimum – usually even longer. In that time, your subconscious will go to work on the issue, and if you're patient, something will almost always bubble to the top. Soon the direction becomes quite clear and the decision practically makes itself. Then you can make a wise decision with confidence and with the peace of mind that comes from knowing you gave the issue due consideration.

An extension of this approach is to adopt it as a "personal policy." If someone (like a salesperson, for example) is pressuring you to make a big decision right now, right away, "before you leave the store," you can look that person in the eye and say, "It's my personal policy to sleep on a decision like this for at least one night." (See Number 27.) If you hold your ground, the salesperson has nothing to argue. The pressure dissipates without any unpleasantries or confrontation. It works!

91.

When you've made a mistake:

1) Note the lessons learned.

2) Forgive yourself.

3) Cut your losses and move on.

Everybody makes mistakes. The question is how we recover from them. If you're beating up on yourself, the best defense is to ask, "Okay, what did I learn from this? What is a potential positive from this? How can I see this as a form of preparation?" When you are able to note at least one lesson learned, you mentally convert the mistake to a learning experience. You may even choose to write down the lesson to reinforce the learning and to help shift your focus from the past to the future.

Then you can let go of the mistake. You can stop tormenting yourself and forgive yourself for not being perfect, doing a better job or being better prepared.

Finally, you can get out of a difficult situation and move ahead. There is no honor in perpetuating a bad decision, especially after you know in your heart that it's a bad decision. And you will only make matters worse if you dig deeper by defending a weak position. Go ahead and cut your losses. Quit second-guessing yourself and don't look back, except to capture the learning. This approach takes some fear out of admitting you were wrong. It helps you find the courage to move on. And it makes past experiences work for you in the future.

92.
Live IN the present, but not just FOR today.

This is about balancing your priorities for the present and the future. To live just for today is rather short sighted. You don't make any plans. You don't prepare for the future. You don't lay the foundation for your dreams. However, if you become too focused on the future, you miss the opportunity to consciously enjoy the precious moments of the present. You whither away today for the promise of tomorrow. You become so focused on the destination that you're oblivious to the journey.

Imagine the broken expectations a person would encounter when they're of age to retire but discover they haven't saved enough money to quit work. Conversely, imagine how hollow one's existence would become if the focus was to delay joy until the mortgage was paid and the kids were out of the house. The result could well be an empty nest with an attractive nest egg, but also a broken relationship between the parents who now have no common goals or connections.

The most prudent approach is to follow a plan. Seek some financial advice. Set up investment or savings plans that help you attain your future goals and desired lifestyle. And then shift your focus to the present so you can enjoy and appreciate it with your loved ones. Regardless of your financial position, there's a multitude of relationship-enhancing things you can do for free. While money may be a tool for present (and future) pleasures, a lack of money is no excuse. Everything it takes to live rich costs nothing. But you pay an immeasurable price when you stumble into your future or surrender your present.

93.
Stop moving, if only for a moment, to appreciate the beauty, the bounty, the blessings all around you.

There's so much around us that is truly spectacular and awesome. And it's so easy to hurry past it all on the way to accomplishing tasks or planning the next big event. Sure, we occasionally stumble across something really good as we go through the motions of our daily routines. But it's a much richer experience when we consciously appreciate the wonders at least as much as we dwell on the toils and tribulations of daily life.

Have you ever been so focused on a job that you missed the beauty of nature and the change of seasons, even though you drove through colored leaves, quiet snow, soft rain and warm summer sun? Have you ever been so focused on achieving or acquiring that you overlooked the abundance already available? Have you ever been so troubled that miracles and blessings seemed to be reserved for the rich and famous?

It's all a matter of perspective. We can allow beauty, bounty and blessings to become background clutter, or we can experience them through the glow of a spotlight. The choice is determined rather simply; it's a question of whether or not we pause to appreciate. That's all. Just a simple pause. We don't have to make radical lifestyle changes, alter obligations or give up anything, unless we want to. All we have to do is make an occasional pit stop for a moment of peace.

94.

At day's end, think of five things for which you are grateful, and plan to do one selfless act tomorrow.

There's power in rituals, especially positive rituals. When you make it an evening routine to recall special moments from the day, you are reminded of your good fortune and joyful encounters. This practice reinforces the memories in your brain and your heart, while your physical body responds again to the pleasant experiences. Additionally, you perpetuate the upward spiral of gratefulness. When you find five good things that happened today, you can't call it a bad day. Yes, sometimes there are some unpleasant things that happen in the course of a good day. But when you're in the habit of recalling good things in the evening, you'll be actively looking for them during the day. When you're looking for happiness, you're likely to find it.

When you consciously plan to do one nice thing tomorrow, you prepare to share joy with others rather than worrying about all the possible things that could go wrong for you. You feel more anticipation and less anxiety. You have yet another way to make it a good day.

95.
Connect with other people – especially those in service positions.

R each out to other people, especially those who provide services. Despite the fact that it's their job and they're getting paid and you're the customer, behave as though they were doing you a favor for free. Immediately you will better appreciate what people do for you and what they say to you – especially if they're your travel agent, secretary, server, shuttle bus driver, mail carrier, delivery person, teacher, clergy, nurse, gas station attendant, etc.

Take travel, for example. You can begin to feel like a person without a country. You're not really connected to anything. You're just encountering strangers, different sights, different foods, different schedules and different routines. Nothing is the same. And then, out of nowhere, someone calls you by name, smiles at you or makes you feel welcome in some way. Or the opposite happens – and you smile at them! You write a thank-you note on a napkin to the waitress, you call the hotel maid by name, you thank the taxi driver, you look the flight attendant in the eye as you hand over your empty pretzel bag. You notice them. You thank them. You wish them a good day. And instantly, you have some kind of connection. You are no longer quite so alone. And you touch other people's lives in the process.

These people make big contributions through generally thankless positions. Yet they are too frequently treated like servants simply because they provide service. When you connect with them, you add meaning to their work. And you add meaning to your routines in the process.

96.
Say, "Maybe you're right" to de-escalate trivial arguments.

When you're in the middle of a heated discussion, it's easy to get caught up in proving a point or finding evidence to support your position. You can quickly become embroiled in winning the argument and in the process, become quite adamant and agitated. Unfortunately, these big disagreements are frequently of small importance. That is, they are not about principles or "mountains," but about some obscure detail or "molehill" that will not make much difference in a day or two. Think of how many times you have argued needlessly over a date, location, number, size or word pronunciation that had no bearing on the issue originally being discussed!

Rather than escalate a difference of opinion, it might be just as well to simply say, "Maybe you're right." This is not an admission that you are wrong, or a concession to the opposing point of view. It simply acknowledges the other person's position and it diffuses the situation. This may be a tough tool to use when you are absolutely convinced that you are right and when you're tempted to continue the argument. (Just 10 more minutes of this discussion and you know you can beat the other person into submission!) Choose to view it as a truce, rather than a surrender. Saying "Maybe you're right" is a tool to end an argument over something that isn't worth arguing about. You can let it go without feeling cowardly. You can stop wasting time and energy on meaningless battles and move ahead to your real priorities.

97.
Live within your means.

B uy only the kind of house and type of car and amenities you can afford. Don't get lured into burdensome payments for the wrong reasons. Financial concerns can quickly nibble into the peace and contentment in your life. They can also prevent you from fully enjoying the very items you purchased.

If you buy a big, expensive house or a fancy car so that someone else will be impressed, you're setting yourself up for disappointment. No one is ever going to be impressed enough for you to rationalize long-term payments you can't really afford.

Instead, make purchases you can afford, and choose items for their intrinsic value as well as any investment value. Set your own course and live within your own means. There is no "instant gratification" in long-term debt. But there is a quiet confidence in knowing that you can afford to live according to the choices you've made.

98.
Park your vehicle a little farther from the building.

M ost of us don't appreciate dings and nicks on our vehicles, yet we're willing to circle the parking lot two or three times to find a nice close parking spot. Meanwhile, we're frequently lamenting that we really need more exercise!

Why do we really search for those close parking spots? It's convenient, but is it really all that important? If you're physically able to walk the distance, why not park a little farther away? You rarely have to race to get a parking spot near the dumpster. And if you park there, your car is at less risk, your body gets more exercise, and it is good for your psyche.

99.
Refrain from telling jokes about sex, drugs or alcohol.

The trouble with these jokes is that you never really know the personal history or values of your audience. You never know what kind of a heart button you will hit with these topics, especially in mixed company. Something that seems very humorous to you can be very hurtful or offensive to someone else. And the negative emotions are then reflected back onto the joke teller. It becomes degrading to you.

Granted, some of these jokes can be quite humorous, when said in good taste. And what each of us says or does in privacy is our own business. But publicly, it's easier, safer and wiser to avoid these topics out of respect for those around you.

People will never think less of you for not telling these jokes. In fact, you're more likely to gain their respect, and more importantly, you'll find more respect for yourself.

100.
Leave something a little better
than you found it.

L et's say that you borrow a hand saw from your neighbor, and while you're using it, you notice that the blade is rather dull. So you have it sharpened before returning it. Or perhaps you picked up a scrap of paper in a park and put it in the trash can. Or maybe you fixed the paper jam in the copy machine at work even though it would have been easier to just use a different copier. These are examples of leaving something a little better than you found it. This mindset doesn't have to result in monumental tasks, although the actions need not be trivial either. The value is in making the donation. Sometimes, people will duly note it and very much appreciate it. Other times, no one may even notice much less care. That's okay. Regardless of how others respond, you remain the beneficiary of the pride and peace that accompany your selfless acts.

When you do these kinds of things, some people may tease you and suggest that you're not making any difference. Don't let that stop you. Your contributions matter. There's also a chance that some day others might start following your example.

101.

Do what you say you will do,
when you say you will do it.
Better yet, under promise and
over deliver.

You build credibility when you do what you say you will do when you say you will do it. You become respectful, responsible, reliable and trustworthy (RRRT) – not only in your interactions with other people, but also in your "interactions" with yourself. Keeping promises you make to others is very important because it builds your interpersonal culture. Keeping promises you make to yourself builds character – a cornerstone of your personal culture.

The "under promise and over deliver" portion of this concept provides opportunities to delight. For example, if you offer to take your spouse's car to get the oil changed and then also get it washed and waxed, you've over delivered in terms of quantity. You can also over deliver sooner than promised. For example, if you promise to deliver something by Friday but then deliver it on Thursday afternoon, you bolster your credibility and enhance your relationships.

Be cautious, however, about under promising too often. If you "pad" your promised delivery dates in order to manipulate people, you won't be taken seriously. The objective is to deliver a little bit ahead of schedule or to deliver a little more quantity than promised. Either way, however, be careful to maintain your standards of quality.

These methods will earn you improved credibility and expanded influence. People will learn that they can rely on you and trust that you will keep your commitments. You'll enjoy personal excellence instead of public excuses.

BONUS ITEM

"In my country ..."

INTRODUCTION: "In my country" is an exercise in determining personal values, passions, beliefs and behaviors. It is a method of defining your personal culture. It also defines interpersonal cultures because it provides a way for you to examine your interactions with other people and make adjustments if you desire.

When you complete this exercise, you will have a better understanding of who you are and how you want to be. You will also have a tool for improving your relationships with others.

Use the phrase "In my country" to help you courageously defend your personal culture and to courteously convey expected behaviors for your interpersonal cultures. For example, you may say to another person, "In my country, we don't belittle people." This is a way to make the expectations clear about how you want to be treated without rudely taking someone to task for their belittling behaviors. You may say, "In my country, we respect other people and their possessions. In my country, we don't call names. In my country, we don't say things designed to deliberately hurt another person. In my country, we respect people's dignity." When you make these statements you confidently display your personal culture. Additionally, you very simply and effectively state the ground rules for your interpersonal relationships.

"In my country" will enrich your life. Try it!

EXERCISE: Imagine that you have just become monarch of a country. You now have supreme authority to make the rules for your country based on your strongest values. All "subjects" are waiting to hear what behaviors you expect and what behaviors are unacceptable in your country.

Assuming that you already have laws of the land, the following items should pertain to beliefs and behaviors that support those laws. (For example, you don't need to write statements like, "In my country we do not kill each other." These rules are assumed to be contained in the laws of the land.)

Below, list a statement next to each bullet point that captures your most passionate beliefs and most desired behaviors. You may add one or two bullet points, if needed.

IN MY COUNTRY WE:
-
-
-
-
-

IN MY COUNTRY WE DO NOT:
-
-
-
-
-

S UMMARY: When you have completed this exercise, you have a guide to help reinforce the beliefs and behaviors you value highly and to discourage people from treating you in ways you find unacceptable.

When people exhibit behavior you value, compliment them. This encourages them to perpetuate the behavior.

Conversely, when people treat you poorly, use "In my country" statements to let them know that their behavior is unacceptable. This is a safe, nonconfrontational way to discourage negative behavior and to establish expectations for future interactions.

INDEX

INTERPERSONAL CULTURE

page

LOVING RELATIONSHIPS

PARENTING AND FAMILY

ON THE JOB

EVERYDAY LIFE

Bonus Item

More Ways To Enrich Your Life?

You're invited to share your ideas about how to enrich
your life (or someone else's life) for inclusion in future
publications from Living Rich, Inc. Please send your
suggestions to us at the address below. We'll be sure to
give you credit for your contributions.

LIVING RICH, INC.
1724 E. Frances St.
Appleton, WI 54911
(920) 731-8599
Ideas@LivingRich.com
www.LivingRich.com

Keynotes, Training and Consulting

For information and inquiries about LIVING RICH™
keynote addresses, training programs and organizational
consulting, please contact Bob Lemke and Karen Diedrich at:

LIVING RICH, INC.
1724 E. Frances St.
Appleton, WI 54911
(920) 731-8599
Inquiries@LivingRich.com
www.LivingRich.com

Additional Copies of <u>*"101 Ways To Enrich Your Life"*</u>

To order additional copies of this book, please send $12.95, plus $3.50 shipping and handling per copy to:

LIVING RICH, INC.
1724 E. Frances St.
Appleton, WI 54911
(920) 731-8599

Number of Copies: _____

@ $12.95 each: $_____

Plus Shipping and Handling*
@ 3.50 each: $_____

Total: $_____

*(*Please note: Shipping is free for orders of 3 or more books sent to the same address. Please make checks payable to **LIVING RICH, INC.**)*

_____
(Name)

_____
(Street Address - please do not list Post Office Boxes)

_____
(City)   (State)   (Zip)

(_____)_____
(Daytime Telephone Number)

— *Thank you* ⌐